Dorothy Stewart is a freelance writer and editor. She has compiled a number of anthologies, including *Women of Prayer* (Loyola Press, 1999). Astonished to find women so poorly represented in traditional anthologies of spiritual writing and prayer, she began the research that led to this collection.

Women
of
Vision

Women
of
Vision

An anthology of spiritual words from
women across the centuries

COMPILED BY DOROTHY STEWART

LOYOLAPRESS.
CHICAGO

LOYOLAPRESS.

3441 N. ASHLAND AVENUE
CHICAGO, ILLINOIS 60657

Revised and expanded edition © 2000 by Loyola Press

Text © 1997 by Dorothy M. Stewart

Original edition published under the title *Women of Spirit* by
Lion Publishing plc, Oxford, England, © 1997 by Lion Publishing plc

Spelling and punctuation have in most cases been conformed to American
usage, and some excerpts have been lightly edited or condensed for readability.

Interior design by Amy Evans McClure

Cover art by Meltem Aktas

Library of Congress Cataloging-in-Publication Data

Women of vision : an anthology of spiritual words from women across the
centuries / compiled by Dorothy Stewart.—Rev. and expanded ed.
    p. cm.
    Rev. ed. of: Women of spirit. Oxford, England : Lion Pub., c1997.
    ISBN 0-8294-1556-4
    1. Christian women—Religious life.   2. Christian women—Conduct
of life.   I. Stewart, Dorothy M.   II. Women of spirit.
BV4527 .W5945 2000
242'.643—dc21

                       00-037098
                       CIP

Printed in the U.S.A.
00 01 02 03 04 / 10 9 8 7 6 5 4 3 2 1

*To my family and friends
and especially to my new family and new friends,
among whom I am delighted to discover
more women of vision*

Contents

Growing in faith, hope, and love   28

God is there for us   79

On death and dying 94

Good out of evil 106

PART THREE: *The Real World*

Our daily work   **127**

Justice for all

Part Four: *Time to Rejoice*

Introduction

Women of Vision seems to follow on quite naturally from *Women of Prayer* (published by Lion in 1993, by Loyola in 1999). So many of the prayers I discovered had been spoken or written by women who were both spirited and spiritual, and I wanted the opportunity to share some more of what they had to say. This is a collection of writings by women who are inspired by God's Spirit and who have spirited natures—as thinkers, preachers, writers, doctors, teachers, mothers, wives, friends: the whole gamut of womankind. Because, after all, the God who made us in her image made us that way!

I have learned much from these women. They hold a mirror up, showing who we are and who we might become. And so I hope their writings will offer inspiration and encouragement. They are us—sometimes more so, sometimes less so. But they are us.

What I have learned is that women of vision know that they need God, and they take time and space to draw near to him. Some prefer to chat with their Heavenly Father, almost like having a friendly phone call home. Others choose the way of silence. All take time to listen for God's answer, whether through prayer or Bible reading, or through sensitivity to God's messages via other people or the world around them.

They aren't perfect. These women know their shortcomings —their bad temper, impatience, lack of humility, whatever it is. They face the sin and failure in their lives and, by offering these things openly to God, they enable him to transform the sin, the failure, and their very selves.

They suffer. The tragedies and miseries of life do not pass them by. Not all are heroines like Aida Skripnikova, imprisoned for her faith, but all have some experience to offer that is common to the general lot of women—illness, surgery, pain, death of friends and relatives, their own impending death. And as they face these things courageously or with honest fear, they reveal the resources of God's Spirit on which they draw.

They care about the world they live in. They have a vision that begins with their own fireside and takes in the whole world. Here are politics, revolution, and militant Christianity. Here is challenge.

Whatever else they may be, they are real women—mainly of our own century, and of these, most are still alive—working out their salvation as God's Spirit enables them. They juggle real lives, just like the rest of us—the concerns and constraints of families (whether elderly relatives, young children, or friends), the daily requirements of work inside and outside the home, church activities, social lives, and all the rest. Most of these women are Western women like me—their stories rang bells with me, and I hope they will chime with you.

You will find words of inspiration, comfort, encouragement, and challenge. But most of all, you will hear the words of women who are prepared to let God's Spirit into their lives in all the reality that is life today.

PART ONE

Keep Close to God

Women of vision keep close to God. Most pray. Some chat in friendly terms; some sit in silence. Some read the Bible, and some watch birds! All consider the time spent with their Heavenly Father as pivotal in their lives. It is from this space that they find the resources they need for their life, their work, and their growth as children of God. And they recognize that growth as needing application and dedication, just as in any garden. As one writer says, we need to keep the path clear!

But paths can easily become overgrown with weeds and so, too, do lives fall into sin and failure. Women of vision are honest about their failings. They recognize the masks we all hide behind—and they take them to God.

There is an assurance and a freedom to be who you are and to become who God wants you to be—fulfilled, filled with joy and his Spirit.

Let us pray

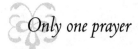 *Only one prayer*

There is really only one possible prayer: Give me to do everything I do in the day with a sense of the sacredness of life. Give me to be in your presence, God, even though I know it only as absence.

May Sarton

Our part

We are only syllables of the perfect Word.

Caryll Houselander

Letting go

I finally decided that I must give up stating the case in my prayers and telling God what I thought he ought to do, and instead just kneel down before God and put it before him simply by saying a name. Like the old peasant who had a bad foot. Since he did not know which was best for him, to be cured, to be lame, to be in pain or out of pain, he just went to church and said, "Lord—foot."

Caryll Houselander

Letting God

In the beginning of my sobriety, I had no idea what "let go and let God" meant. It's only five words, and I understand it very well today, but at that time I was directing God, telling him what I wanted. I probably gave him a list.

Betty Ford

Don't give up

Sustained efforts are necessary. If you spend your time pulling down with one hand what you build up with the other, you will never achieve anything. This is not the work of a day but a lifetime, so it is no use just making one or two isolated efforts; you have to persevere. Remember what the Apocalypse says: "Be thou faithful unto death and I will give thee the crown of life." Nothing can be had for nothing. The kingdom of God suffers violence. And what about you? You don't mind making a few attempts, but to keep the effort up costs too much altogether!

Saint Julie Billiart

Remove the mask

A Christian's relationship with God is just as stormy and precarious as any human relationship. It is just as hard to remove your mask and open up to God as it is to those around you, and the fear of rejection is more intense because it is an infinite, eternal, ultimate rejection. I will argue that this fear is groundless. It arises mainly because, I feel, we read too much of ourselves into God.

Elizabeth Stuart

Like a child to her father

The simple person goes straight to God like a child to her father. It is easy for her to draw near to him for she is so direct in her prayer, and God on his side loves to talk with one who is as candid and simple as a child.

Saint Julie Billiart

Eyes shut or eyes open?

Some people find it easier than others to sustain a personal relationship with God through prayer. Prayer can, however, become a mere symptom of our brokenness. It is easy to use prayer to try to impose upon God our own desires, concerns, and opinions and to justify our alienated condition. We avoid the guilt and frustration of facing our shared responsibility for most of the misery in the world by turning in upon ourselves and concerning ourselves only with our own salvation. When we hear the words "Let us pray," what do most of us do? We bow our heads, close our eyes, perhaps kneel down, and immediately start to think about our own needs and pet causes. We turn in upon ourselves and we set the agenda. We are afraid to let God in, in case he shows us something or someone we do not want to see and calls us into situations we would rather avoid. People who seek wholeness and have a desire to communicate God's grace to others will, metaphorically at least, pray with their eyes open to allow God to direct their eyes toward what forms their shadow side, [which is] in need of love and acceptance, and also toward people and situations calling for his healing grace.

Elizabeth Stuart

Pray with your whole heart

Prayer is naught else but a yearning of soul. When it is practiced with the whole heart, it has great power. It makes a sour heart sweet, a sad heart merry, a poor heart rich, a foolish heart wise, a timid heart courageous, a sick heart well, a blind heart full of vision, a cold heart ardent. For it draws down the great God into the little heart; it drives the hungry soul up to the plenitude of God; it brings together these two lovers, God and the soul, in a wondrous place where they speak much of love.

Saint Mechthild of Magdeburg

Where shall I find God?

Where shall I find God? In myself. That is the true
Mystical Doctrine. But then I myself must be in a state for
him to come and dwell in me. This is the whole aim of the
Mystical life, and all Mystical rules in all time and coun-
tries have been laid down for putting the soul into such a
state.

Florence Nightingale

Our Father

May his name be always hallowed in heaven and on earth, and may his will always be done in me. Amen.

God has made me understand what great things we ask when we say this heavenly prayer. May he be blessed forever, since it is certain I never imagined this prayer comprised such great mysteries. You have already seen how it includes in itself the whole way of perfection, from the very commencement, till God engulfs the soul in himself, and makes her drink abundantly of the fountain of Living Water, which flows at the end of the road. It seems our Lord was pleased to make us, sisters, understand the great consolations contained therein, and that this prayer is exceedingly useful for persons who cannot read. Did they understand it well, they might gain much instruction from it, and much comfort to themselves.

Saint Teresa of Ávila

Pray with your lips

As to prayer, I will say but this one word. When you cannot reap, take with violence; that is, pray at least with your lips, when you cannot with your heart.

Blessed Baptista Varani

Wisdom through prayer

"When we ask our father for bread, he does not give a stone; nor if we ask him for fish will he give a serpent." Much less will he refuse us what is necessary to make us pleasing to him, if we seek or desire nothing but by true love to be faithful to him. O prayer, prayer, you are able to obtain all things! Oh, how does it come to pass, my Lord, that this omnipotent thing (as some of your dear servants term it), prayer, should be so unknown? Yea, and even by those whom you term the salt of the earth, it is condemned (I mean mental prayer) at least for the practice of poor simple women, for whom they hold it to be above all things most dangerous. Surely a want of that wisdom, which the saints did gain by prayer, is the cause why custom and opinion take the place of true reason for the most part in this world.

Dame Gertrude More

Don't hang up—hang on

Waiting for the answer

It is during our busy, noisy times—when we rush about, making as much noise as we can—that things go wrong. We do not stop to think, let alone tackle problems.

When we want advice from someone and telephone to ask for it, do we quickly tell this person what our difficulty is and then hang up the receiver before getting a reply? That is our usual attitude when we ask God for help. We hang up quickly and start rushing about again, instead of being quiet and waiting for a reply.

It is in the quietness that we shall get some sort of answer and peace of mind. This is a difficult thing to do at times, but it will come with practice if we can start now. Every time we talk to God we should take a few minutes and listen inwardly.

Victoria Lidiard

Practicing the presence of God

The only way I can learn to practice the presence of God is
to do it, and one thing I am very sure of for myself is that
to sit quietly before God doing nothing, only fixing the
will gently on some expressive words like "O God, I want
thee" or "Father" or "Here am I and here are you" makes a
world of difference. Just as lying in the sun doing nothing,
surrendering your body to it, with the sun blazing down on
you, affects your body and your senses, so this surrendering
of the soul to that transforming Power affects the soul, and
I believe that as truly as the sun changes the color of your
skin, so that Power changes you at the center.

Florence Allshorn

Staying awake

Increasingly, prayer seems to be a waiting—and often, a goalless waiting. It is simply an end in itself. If some resolution, insight, or peace comes, it comes as a gift, not as something I have angled for. I was at a loss to explain this to anyone until I remembered that the French for "to wait" is *attendre.* Then it became clear that waiting is giving one's complete and undivided attention to the present moment, to the person or situation one wants to "hold in the Light," to the object before one's eyes, or to the word arising in one's mind. To keep vigil is to be awake, waiting, attentive.

Kate Compston

Silence

A woman who neglects silence brings only a distracted
heart and a preoccupied mind to her prayer and, instead of
deriving new strength from it, she only makes herself guilty
before God by going to him with a heart taken up by trifles.
Intimate conversation with God is easily stifled if you do
not first put an end to exterior chatter; but if you love
silence and keep it well, your heart will be a temple where
God will dwell. He will make his will known to you there.
He will receive your constant adoration and will converse
familiarly with you.

Saint Julie Billiart

 *In the dark*

I no longer panic at dry or so-called dark periods. I learned long ago that if those times didn't come, we wouldn't be normal. How we feel—how I feel "spiritually"—seems less and less relevant. What matters is that God is constant. He is the only constant anywhere in the world.

Eugenia Price

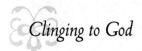 *Clinging to God*

It is good to have some desolation in prayer; it makes us cling to God.

Saint Julie Billiart

Trust—like a cat

No sooner had he [her cat, Jones] jumped on my lap than he relaxed, he went limp—happily, deliciously limp—and indicated by various signs known to me that he wanted his ears scratched. That done, he went to sleep. I ought to be able to treat God as my cat treats me; only, whereas my cat is deluded about my omnipotence, I am right about God's.

Caryll Houselander

God keeps his promises

A verse from the book of Proverbs says, "God keeps every promise he makes." I have found in my life, in every circumstance, that this is true. He has never disappointed me, and the nearer I get to him, the deeper I enter into his life, then I find his promises unfolding like leaves in spring, and there at the center the kernel which is his everlasting love—his promise fulfilled in me and for me. Draw closer to him now. You will not be disappointed. The closer you come, the more you will be able to receive, and the more you will have to share.

Margaret Cundiff

Being God's friend

I've caught on, I think, to something of what St. Paul meant when he wrote that we were to "pray without ceasing." My devotional times are not as scheduled as they once were, but then I was knocking myself out trying to be a "good and faithful servant." You see, I've learned that Jesus meant it when he said that he would no longer call his disciples servants, but friends. I have a very simple goal now: to be God's friend.

Eugenia Price

Offertory and consecration

I am the cold insipid water ready to be poured
into the chalice.
Let me be put into the wine like the drop of water
at this Mass.
Let me be flooded through with the strength, the color,
the splendor of your Being, as the colorless water is flooded
with the crimson of the wine.
At the words of consecration let me be changed,
changed by the miracle of your love into yourself.
In the chalice of your sacrifice, lift me to Our Father.

Caryll Houselander

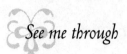# See me through

I always told God, I'm going to hold steady on you, an' you've got to see me through.

Harriet Tubman

A vision on the eve of martyrdom

We were just beginning the struggle, when there came toward us a man of so prodigious a stature that he reached to the very top of the amphitheater. Having ordered silence, he said: "If this Egyptian conquer her, he shall slay her with his sword; if she overcome him, she shall receive this branch and the golden apples."

Then he withdrew. Thereupon I grappled with the Egyptian. I had placed my foot upon his head so as to crush it. Loud acclamations from the people rent the air; my companions sang a hymn of triumph. I went up to the person who appeared as the master of the games; he received me with a smile of delight, he gave me the promised prize and, affectionately embracing me, said: "Peace be with thee, my daughter." And while the accents of joy resounded all around, I proceeded toward the gate called Laura-Vivaria. At this moment, my vision vanished. I understood that the combat in the amphitheater was to be not so much against the wild beasts as with the devil. But, at the same time, I was cheered on by the assurance that victory would crown my struggle.

Saint Perpetua

Growing in faith, hope, and love

Bible reading

Once I had considered Bible reading a dull chore. College courses in which we studied the Bible as literature had not changed that concept.

But after I made an act of committing my life to God, gradually for me, the Bible underwent a transformation. I wanted to read the Bible because it told me so much about the character and ways of God. I found myself eager to know how he dealt with men and women in every imaginable circumstance.

I came to understand that God means that all lives be lived in cooperation with him. His friendship, his plans for us, his riches are awaiting us, provided we want him in our lives. The riches of grace must be claimed.

Catherine Marshall LeSourd

Letting things fall

Possess yourself as much as you possibly can in peace; not by any effort, but by letting all things fall to the ground which trouble or excite you. This is no work, but is, as it were, a setting down of a fluid to settle that has become turbid through agitation.

Madame Guyon

Dangerous saints

A course of reading brought to me a sense of the quality of service given to the world by people like the Lady Julian of Norwich, Catherine of Siena, the Quaker Saints, Josephine Butler, and that great host of dedicated lives. My everyday trade union work took on a deeper significance. The doing of ordinary, everyday things became lit up with that inner light of the Spirit that gave one strength and effectiveness—strength to meet defeat with a smile, to face success with a sense of responsibility, to be willing to do one's best without thought of reward, to bear misrepresentation without giving way to futile bitterness.

Saint Teresa declared that "there are only two duties required of us—the love of God and the love of our neighbor—and the surest sign of discovering whether we observe these duties is the love of our neighbor." And a great scholar has asserted that this love of God is not an emotion, although that may be experienced; it is a principle of action, it reinforces effort; it demands that we do something, not merely talk or feel sympathetic. We've got to use the new strength or it will break us.

That is the vital difference between those who drift with the stream, as I did at first, and those who, like the great souls down the ages, inspire, revive, and strengthen the corporate life of their generation. Most of them are

treated by their contemporaries as dangerous—and they
are, to systems outworn and hampering.

Margaret Bondfield

Learning faith, hope, and love

When we first begin to follow Christ's way of life, our knowledge of it is very embryonic and elementary, and yet we are inclined to think that we have the whole secret. We regard it as unnecessary to train ourselves in those sensitizing obediences that are the condition of receiving the heavenly grace that alone brings the flower and the fruit. Faith, hope, and love have to be learned with infinite patience through a long time. They are the demands of a Creator who knew what he would have us be. We cannot pursue them feebly and attain in the Christian life. They are supreme ends, which we cannot allow to be crowded out of our lives by a host of lesser purposes.

Florence Allshorn

The disciplines of life

What have I learned in these last six years? That Spirit-motivated disciplines facilitate the Christian walk. Oh, I'm not discounting all the warm feelings along the road, when I've sung Jesus-songs and held hands and the rest. But our sensuous age forgets that feelings come and feelings leave you, but the disciplines of life are what get you to where you want to go.

Anne Ortlund

A new relationship with Mary

We have heard, endlessly and wearisomely, all the reasons why Mary "doesn't work" as a metaphor for our times and for our generation. We have heard that Mary is too passive, too much of a people pleaser, too weak, too virginal, too pure, too easily shaped, too obedient, too good to be true. All these complaints seem thin and beside the point.

"Immensity, cloistered in thy dear womb," wrote John Donne in his sonnet on the Annunciation. In earlier centuries, Christian poets, storytellers, and playwrights added constantly to the wealth of material that could be drawn on for devotion; they wove new cloth for our contemplation and prayer. Something much like that is needed for our contemporary imagination. By grace we can experience a comparable flowering of religious and spiritual imagination, not only for creative artists, but in the depths of our own hearts. Yes, we moderns are capable of a new kind of relationship to Mary, one with a level of sophistication that corresponds to our new biblical and philosophical understanding. Even for people like us, who have heard and seen it all, it is possible to discover Mary by all her many titles, shedding graces in our Christian lives.

Emilie Griffin

Keep the path clear

God is always pressing toward us with love, but he needs the open path of our basic commitment in order to care for us as he longs to do. We decide whether or not we will clear the path or keep it cluttered with doubts.

Eugenia Price

On receiving a gift

The Lord said: "Is it well to repay friendship with harshness, or would one put snow in a cold vessel, unless one wished to make it colder still? Therefore, even if this queen has given you what she has sent from no warmth of heart, still it is your part to accept it in a spirit of humility and charity, and to pray for her that she may be enkindled with the fire of divine love. For it is written: 'Let your abundance supply their want.' And no good work is ever forgotten by God."

Saint Bridget of Sweden

A gift of faith

A brilliant light of hope and peace filled my soul. At once, I knew not how, the terror fled away. A deep conviction came to me that my life was accepted by God. This unusual experience at the outset of my medical career has had a lasting and marked effect on my whole life. To me it was a revealed experience of Truth, a direct vision of the great reality of spiritual existence, as irresistible as it is incommunicable. I shall be grateful to the last day of my life for this great gift of faith.

Elizabeth Blackwell

Awareness of God

The intensity of prayer is not measured by time, but by the reality and depth of one's awareness of unity with God. I learned to look on prayer not as a means of influencing the Creator in my favor, but as an awareness of the presence of God—everywhere.

Margaret Bondfield

The hardest lesson

True resignation is the hardest lesson in the whole school of Christ. It is the oftenest taught and the latest learned. The submission of yesterday does not exonerate us from the resignation of today.

Hannah More

Ready to obey

God must be sought and seen in his providences; it is not our actions in themselves considered which please him, but the spirit in which they are done, more especially the constant ready obedience to every discovery of his will, even in the minutest things, and with such a suppleness and flexibility of mind as not to adhere to anything, but to turn and move in any direction where he shall call.

Madame Guyon

Guard the city of your soul

I desire to see you a true guardian of the city of your soul.
This city has many gates! They are three—Memory,
Intellect, and Will—and our Creator allows all of them to
be battered, and sometimes opened by violence, except one,
that is, Will. So it happens at times that the intellect sees
nothing but shadows; the memory is occupied with vain
and transitory things. None of these gates is in our own
free possession, except only the Gate of Will. This belongs
to our liberties, and has Freewill for its Watch.

Let us strive to hold good and zealous watch, keeping at
the side of our Watch Freewill the dog Conscience, who
when anyone comes to the gate must awake Reason by its
barking, that she may discern whether it be friend or foe:
so that the watch may let friends enter, ordering good and
holy inspirations to do their work, and may drive away the
foes, locking the Gate of Will, that it consent not to admit
the evil thoughts that come to the gate every day. And
when your city shall be demanded of you by the Lord, you
can give it up, sound and adorned with true and royal
virtues, thanks to his grace.

Saint Catherine of Siena

Seven jewels in a crown of patience

The first stone in this crown is a *jasper*, gained for you by him who spoke of you contemptuously, saying it would better become you to spin than to dispute about the Scriptures. The *sapphire* was won for you by him who spoke friendly words to your face and robbed you of credit behind your back. The man to thank for the *emerald* is he who accused you of saying things you never said or thought. A *pearl* was placed in your crown by one you heard slander a friend of God, an injury that grieved you more than if it had been aimed at yourself. When you returned blessing for words of bitterness, you gained a *topaz*. The *diamond* was set in your crown by him who struck you to the ground, a wrong you bore patiently, praying for him. The *carbuncle* was gained when the servant brought you false tidings of your son Karl's death, and you heard them patiently, submitting your will to the will of God. Be steadfast, my daughter, for there are gems yet wanting to make your crown perfect.

Saint Bridget of Sweden, recounting her vision of Saint Agnes

If they had known

I freed thousands of slaves. I could have freed thousands more, if they had known they were slaves.

Harriet Tubman

Advice to a religious person

Do not sleep in sloth and negligence, for the kingdom suffers violence, and the violent bear it away. You must guard continually against this fatal sleep to which many religious persons abandon themselves, who, forgetful of their first fervor, perform all their works without attention. You know the habit of goats—when one leaps over a fence all the rest follow. Thus these religious observe their rules and ceremonies. They see what others do and follow them, but without considering why they act thus. Such souls are like asses, which are sometimes employed by their masters to carry wines and yet only drink water. Now this is exactly what happens to religious persons who have this spirit of slumber; they carry burdens that cause them great fatigue and derive from them but little fruit. As matter without form is neither useful nor beautiful, so likewise good works performed without a definite intention are little pleasing to God or beneficial to the doer. The work may be praiseworthy in itself, but the want of an intention deprives it of form and renders it fruitless; so that they are but fools who act in this manner. In place of imitating their folly, strive, my child, to follow the example of the wise and prudent, who consider God alone in their works, whether they be great or small, doing everything to please him and suffering everything for love of him.

Blessed Baptista Varani

Fly toward God

Never divide into two years what can be done in one. Walk, run, fly in the path of God. The just walk, the wise run, the loving fly toward the enjoyment of the divine Majesty. You will be wrong to walk if you can run, and to run if you can fly, because time is short. The same thing happens to the soul if it does not grow in virtue. It begins by "I believe in God" and will end by "the resurrection of the body," that is, the cares of this world. If you wish to make great progress, fear God and love your enemies.

Blessed Baptista Varani

Thou shalt not worry

My good Master said to me these words full of tenderness:
"It is my will that thou shouldst not vex thyself."

Lucie Christine

Keeping a journal record

The first practical step for me, then, in acquiring religious efficiency is to make an account of myself, of my supply of time and my manner of using it. Remember, time is really the most wonderful of God's gifts, for when it ceases for us, all else ceases with it, that is, in the sense of meriting or gaining anything for heaven. In this all men are equal: no one has more than twenty-four hours a day. Time flows on in a constant stream and cannot be halted in its course. Our day is, in a way, laid out for us by obedience, and our very manner of life suggests a certain routine, but we must go farther and find out if there are not some little "inbetweenities," as someone has aptly styled these spare moments, and we will be surprised and astonished at the number wasted, due either to mismanagement or sheer carelessness.

But records do more than this. "Know thyself." Self-knowledge is the information they give.

Sister Mary Cecilia

Cooperating with grace

Grace increases in proportion as man makes use of it. Hence it is evident that God gives man from day to day all that he needs, no more and no less, and to each according to his condition and capacity. All this he does for the love and benefit of man; because we are so cold and negligent in our endeavors, and because the instinct of the spirit is to arrive quickly at perfection, it seems as if grace were insufficient. Yet it is not so, and the fault is wholly ours in not cooperating with the grace already received, which therefore ceases to increase.

Saint Catherine of Genoa

Facing the facts

All sinners together

Remember, my dear, I give advice that is rather more human and sympathetic than orthodox. The root reason is that I dare not give unctuous and rigid counsel to anyone because I am so profoundly and always conscious of being a sinner myself, not in imagination, but in reality and with a ghastly accumulation of irrefutable proof. Consequently I dare not say to people, "You must do this or that because it would be right," knowing full well that if I were in their shoes I would do something very much more wrong than they should.

Caryll Houselander

Down-to-earth holiness

The Holy Spirit never inspires anything contrary to the love of God. I pray God to grant you perseverance. What you need is patience, for in patience you shall preserve your soul.

Blessed Julian of Norwich, to Margery Kempe

If Jesus is for us

The church is full of all sorts of people, sinners true
enough, like me; I know that. I know the promises I make
and fail miserably to keep, my bad temper, my impatience. I
know well enough, and I have enough people who draw my
attention to them frequently—which doesn't always help
my temper either! Being a minister in a small church in a
small town means a rather goldfish-like existence; nothing
escapes attention, particularly what I am doing, saying, or
looking like! And that goes for all those who dare to call
themselves the friends of Jesus. The wonderful thing is,
though, Jesus offers his friendship and his love to sustain us
day by day. It doesn't matter what others think about us,
whether they consider us beyond the pale or not, whether
they can point their fingers at our shortcomings and failures. What matters is that Jesus loves us and is not ashamed
to be called our friend. He understands us, knows our
weaknesses, and will help us.

Margaret Cundiff

Christ in the sinner

I saw too the reverence that everyone must have for a sinner; instead of condoning his sin, which is in reality his utmost sorrow, one must comfort Christ who is suffering in him. And this reverence must be paid even to those sinners whose souls seem to be dead, because it is Christ, who is the life of the soul, who is dead in them; they are his tombs, and Christ in the tomb is potentially the risen Christ. For the same reason, no one of us who has fallen into mortal sin himself must ever lose hope.

Caryll Houselander

Chance after chance

As I look at my life I see areas of hardness, of shallow "promises, promises" which never get anywhere, areas of preoccupation with my own life, with what I want to do, what I want to be. I allow these things to put a stranglehold on my effective ministry, but it's often not until I feel the life being squeezed from me that I come to my senses. It is often a very painful process, and could have been avoided if I had taken more care.

The joy is, though, that the sower does not sow once, but over and over again, year in and year out. He never gives up, because he is confident of a harvest. In the book of Isaiah there is a promise which I hold on to, and it is this: "My word is like the snow and the rain that come down from the sky to water the earth. . . . So also will be the word that I speak—it will not fail to do what I plan for it; it will do everything I send it to do" (Isaiah 55:10–11).

God does not give up on me or you; we get chance after chance. But how sad that we waste those chances so often, when we could have been beautiful and useful if only we had listened and received what he had for us.

Margaret Cundiff

Run and ask forgiveness

"Lie down and be discouraged" is always our temptation.
Our feeling is that it is presumptuous, and even almost
impertinent, to go at once to the Lord after having sinned
against him. It seems as if we ought to suffer the conse-
quences of our sin first for a little while, and endure the
accusings of our conscience; and we can hardly believe that
the Lord can be willing at once to receive us back into loving fellowship with himself.

The fact is that the same moment that brings the consciousness of sin ought to bring also the confession and
the consciousness of forgiveness.

Hannah Whitall Smith

The basis of new life

The world of nature gives us an inner satisfaction when we see how all the waste and surplus, the abortive beginnings and the mistakes, are used as the basis of new life. We know, too, that we can never be satisfied unless human evil—the evil will, *sin*—is dealt with in a similar way. Not just conquered and slain like a dragon, but so purged, so transformed that it is able to be used once again as material for living. That is what redemption must accomplish; and it always must involve sacrificing and dying.

Mary F. Smith

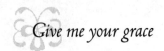

Give me your grace

Lord, you know me. I am so set in my ways.

I am stubborn, self-centered, and so sure I know it all.

I must make you angry.

Yet you love me, you are sorry for me, you want to give me
   so much.

Give me the grace to admit when I am wrong,

to turn from myself and accept your love, your way, your
   will,

today and always.

Margaret Cundiff

Love without strings

For many people, especially those alone and isolated, the closest friend they have is not a human being but an animal, and animals too can become the mediators of God's grace. It did not matter to me what my own dog did—ignore me, bite me, prefer the company of someone else, refuse to do what he was told. I loved him far too much to be angry with him. One day, when we were watching television together, I realized that just as there were no strings attached to my love for George so there are no strings to God's love for us. This had a profound effect upon me—it healed my constant disabling guilt and fear at being a "sinner" and deserving God's wrath and set me free to become less preoccupied with myself and more concerned with others.

Elizabeth Stuart

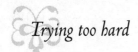 *Trying too hard*

My carefully book-learned principles of childcare col-
lapsed when I saw such successful results coming out of
comparative neglect. In mothering, as in Christianity, we
mess things up by striving too earnestly, obeying too literally, working too scrupulously: we cannot replace grace
by effort.

Margaret Hebblethwaite

God wants to forgive

A little girl once asked whether the Lord Jesus always forgives us for our sins as soon as we asked him, and I had said, "Yes, of course he does."

"Just as soon?" she repeated doubtingly.

"Yes," I replied, "the very minute we ask, he forgives us."

"Well," she said deliberately, "I cannot believe that. I should think he would make us feel sorry for two or three days first. And then I should think he would make us ask him a great many times, and in a very pretty way too, not just in common talk. And I believe that is the way he does, and you need not try to make me think he forgives me right at once, no matter what the Bible says."

She only said what most Christians think, and what is worse, what most Christians act on, making their discouragement and their very remorse separate them infinitely farther off from God than their very sin would have done. Yet it is so totally contrary to the way we like our children to act toward us that I wonder how we ever could have conceived such an idea of God.

How a mother grieves when a naughty child goes off alone in despairing remorse and doubts her willingness to forgive; and how, on the other hand, her whole heart goes

out in welcoming love to the repentant little one who runs
to her at once and begs forgiveness! Surely our God felt this
yearning love when he said to us, "Return, ye backsliding
children, and I will heal your backslidings."

Hannah Whitall Smith

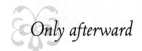

Only afterward

Through the resurrection of Jesus, God reveals that he is
the one who brings life from death and wholeness from
brokenness. The important fact so often overlooked in this
revelation is that wholeness, healing, and salvation come
only after and through the human experience of alienation,
suffering, and death. One cannot be completely healed
until one has been utterly broken.

Elizabeth Stuart

Witness through weakness

If we look at various passages in Scripture, we see that Jesus makes some of his strongest points through those who would have been regarded as the weaker members in the society of the day—the healing of the blind man, the man who was sick of the palsy, the man with the withered hand, and Legion, for example. All these people would have been seen as social outcasts, the nonachievers, and yet Jesus shows us what can be achieved by faith. If God gave me such a clear message, then it suggested that if he wanted me to witness through my weakness, the obstacles confronting me would be overcome.

Lin Berwick

God in our failure

If you have ever been sickened by the crumbling of some enterprise into which you had put all your best effort and the love of your heart, you are caught up in the fellowship of Christ's death and resurrection, whether or not you thought of your experience in that way. God has dealt with our failure by himself becoming a failure in Jesus Christ and so healing it from the inside. That is why we can meet him in our failure; it is a sure place for finding him, since he has claimed it. So central is failure to the Easter mystery that a person who has never grappled with it could scarcely claim to be Christ's friend and follower.

Maria Boulding

Shipwrecked in the port of religion?

O God, most gracious and full of goodness, Father of infinite mercies, I am a sheep from among the hundred, who had quitted thy fold to seek bad pasturage, where I have fed on bitter herbs and poisonous husks. After three years passed in this sad wandering, I desire with all my heart to return to thee. O God of sweetness and mercy, only source of true peace, receive me, then, with charity, take me on thy merciful shoulders. O generous and faithful Shepherd, who has given thy life for thy sheep, bring me back into thy dear fold and turn not thy face away from me. O my sweet Jesus, do not permit me to be shipwrecked in the very port of religion after having struggled so hard to withdraw from the stormy ocean of the world. Remember, O my well-beloved, not what I have done, but what I have wished to do for thy honor. My Jesus, I am the poor publican spoken of in the gospel; shame for my sins hinders me from raising my head, and the confusion caused by them makes me not dare to look up to heaven. Like him, I cast my eyes on the ground and strike my breast, saying: "O God, be merciful to me, a sinner."

Blessed Baptista Varani

PART TWO

Real Lives, Real Pain

Women of vision live in the real world. Tragedy doesn't pass them by or bounce off some supernatural protective shield.

They're in there—in the cancer ward, at the husband's or child's graveside, in the mental hospital, in prison, flat on their back with a slipped disc—suffering just like anyone else, asking the hard questions, and drawing on their faith for the answers and the strength to get through.

Not all their ideas or methods may appeal to you. These women are as different as you and I. But the pattern is still clear: Wherever we lean on God, he'll be right there for us.

No insurance policy—only grace

 *Being human*

"If you are going to live, you are going to love; and if you are going to love, you are going to be hurt and broken."
To be human is to be broken.

Anonymous, quoted by Elizabeth Stuart

The grace to endure

We reviewed our theological position, which we had frequently discussed, namely, that "the rain falls on the just and on the unjust." We do not expect God's special intervention for us. We live now as we always have—by the natural law of cause and effect. It is a part of the human condition. If you are stricken with a fatal disease, you will die. It's that simple—and that terrible. Faith in God provides the grace to endure.

JoAnn Kelley Smith

Forgivable failures

Eventually my social worker referred us to a children's therapist. When I went to the child clinic, the sight of all those
other little terrors toddling about the floor made me feel so
ill that I burst into tears, and when this happened for the second time running, the social worker decided *I* needed help.

The therapist's advice was meant to be nondirective,
while in fact it had a clear moral undertone of a sort I did
not like. "You and your husband are both very religious,
I gather," she said. "How does that affect your feelings
about Dominic?"

"It helps," I said.

The therapist looked surprised and immediately
changed the subject. I had given the wrong answer—I was
meant to say it instilled guilt feelings. But I had probably
found more solace than anywhere else in the Christian
understanding that we all fail, that my failures in the field
where I most wanted to succeed were not only forgivable
but to be expected.

Margaret Hebblethwaite

Nothing is your own

Despise the world and yourself and all its joys, possessing your kingdom as a thing lent to you, and not your own. For well you know that not life nor health nor riches nor honor nor dignity nor lordship is your own. Were they yours, you could possess them in your own way. But in such an hour a man wishes to be well, he is ill; or living, and he is dead; or rich, and he is poor; or a lord, and he is made a servant and vassal. All this is because these things are not his own, and he can hold them only insofar as may please God who has lent them to him. Very simpleminded, then, is the man who holds the things of another as his own. He is really a thief and worthy of death. Therefore I beg you that, as the Wise, you should act like a good servant, made God's steward by God; possessing all things as merely lent to you.

Saint Catherine of Siena

Give me courage

Lord Jesus,
When you rode into Jerusalem on Palm Sunday,
you knew it was the road to the cross,
yet you still took that road.
Give me the courage to take the road I should today,
whatever it may mean, wherever it may lead.
May I travel trustfully and obediently through this day,
content to leave tomorrow in your safe hands,
and tonight rest in your peace.

Margaret Cundiff

Not alone

Christians cannot expect to have charmed lives. One of my initial reactions to John's death was identical to that of the majority of people who face tragedy—"Why should this happen to me?" Now I see the answer to that question is "Why not?" Being a Christian is not a sort of insurance policy. We must take the knocks as well and as much as anybody else. Christian happiness cannot be rooted in other people, in health or worldly fortunes. It must rest in the assurance that we have a heavenly Father who will see that all things work together for good.

My greatest comfort in the blackest days was the very presence and understanding of Christ himself, and the tremendous sense of being part of the Body of Christ, with a great awareness of the love and prayers of the dedicated Christians who stood by me. Their prayers upheld and carried me along where alone I would have fallen.

Even in my times of blackest despair, I sensed that I was not alone. Jesus never left me for one second. He was always there in the darkness, almost as real as a physical presence. Always there was the knowledge that he had endured an even greater darkness for our sakes, and he understood and had experienced death in a way we never shall, because he has conquered death. In my suffering I caught a tiny glimpse of part of the cost of our salvation.

Barbara Piller

Bad times—and good

Jesus, I praise you because I have known sickness and pain,
I praise you because I have known poverty, failure, and
  contempt,
I praise you because I have been falsely accused and
  misjudged,
I praise you because I have suffered the parting of death,
I praise you because I have lived in sordid surroundings,
and I praise you for your goodness in bringing me to a
  happy home
and giving the Faith to my friend.
Grant that I may always sip from the Chalice I am unworthy
  to drink from,
and support me every moment with the strong enfolding
  arm of your Love.

Caryll Houselander

Unshakable foundation

My experience of mental illness was not in vain. I have learned to treat the whole subject of mental health with a new respect. My wild ideas about "loony bins" and the mentally sick have been drastically revised, and it has been a great help to talk things through with a Christian friend who is a psychiatrist. Not only can I understand a little better the reasons for certain methods of treatment, but I also feel I understand my illness and its causes a little better.

I was on "drugs" for over a year: tranquilizers and sleeping tablets by the bottle. I have heard some Christians say a Christian should not need to take drugs. Was I failing God then? Only if I also believe that Christians should never have breakdowns, and that I cannot accept. A breakdown is an illness with causes and symptoms like any other illness. If the doctor prescribes aspirin for influenza and I take those, then why should I not take tranquilizers and sleeping tablets to relieve the symptoms of mental illness?

So where some would look only for the harmful effects of psychiatry and drugs I can see only blessing and fruitfulness.

The breakdown has given me a foundation deep within my spiritual experience that is unshakable, tested as the onslaught of the illness stormed at the defenses of my faith and tore away my immature, untested ideas, whittling my experience of God down to its basics. I look back and claim the promise of John 10 that no one can snatch me from God's hand. No experience can be worse than the agony of that breakdown. I can face the future secure in God's grip.

Mary Endersbee

Communion

He is still on earth in the host,
He is crucified in the Mass
And in my Communion
Rises again in me.

Whatever I have to suffer,
However hardly I die to self,
He will rise in me.

However numbed I have been
By even the greatest sorrow,
The cruelest disappointment,
He will rise again in me.

Caryll Houselander

A small and imperfect instrument

Yesterday, my traveling day. As we passed through M——,
I adored my Lord present in that town, and then seeing all
the railway lines crossing each other in that place I thought:
How like this is to the image of a soul who receives special
graces. This little town, being favorably situated, has been
chosen in the general interest as center of communications,
and all these lines cross it in order to go *beyond it.* Thus the
soul to whom God has given as a special grace the need to
adore and make reparation, and whom he deigns to aid in
that way by continual and especial helps, should not think
that such graces are for herself alone. She must have a
wider and juster outlook and reflect that the fruits of those
graces are given for the sake of many others, and besides,
that God chooses a *little* soul for his great designs, that all
may know that it is really *he* who operates the good, and
that he can do all it pleases him to do with a small and
imperfect instrument.

Lucie Christine

God carries us

When we carry a very heavy load, our strength gives way;
but if we throw that load into the water it immediately
loses its weight and we can sustain it with one finger. It is
the same with our sorrows; if we carry them alone we are
crushed by them, but let us only cast them into the immensity of God, and from that moment it is scarcely we who
carry them. It is we who, together with our sorrows, are
carried in the bosom of God, in the bosom of his mercy.

Lucie Christine

God is there for us

Words of strength

He did not say, "You shall not be tempest-tossed, you shall not be work-weary, you shall not be discomforted." But he said, "You shall not be overcome."

Blessed Julian of Norwich

Jesus makes the difference

In searching for God's purpose—the reasons behind events—I saw that whenever I had come to Jesus stripped of pretensions, with a needy spirit, ready to listen to him and to receive what he had for me, he had met me at my point of need. He can make the difference in every human situation.

The word *impossible* melts away with him. He knows no defeat and can turn every failure and frustration into unexpected victory. He can reverse a doctor's grim prognosis. With him, a seemingly dark and desolate future becomes a joyous new life.

I know all this to be true because I have lived it. I have met God at moments when the straight road turns, and he has picked me up, wiped away my tears, and set me back on the path of life.

Catherine Marshall LeSourd

Faith reaffirmed

When I was hospitalized for my mastectomy, I thought,
this could be it, and only God can help me. Through
prayer, I let go and turned it over. This was before I knew I
was alcoholic, before I had ever heard these phrases.
Tension dissolved, my mind and my whole body relaxed, it
was as though a huge weight had been lifted from me, as
though a light had gone on. God was in my life. He would
take care of me, and I was going to be all right. That day,
my faith in God was reaffirmed in such a strong way that it
has never really faltered since.

Betty Ford

Not broken

During the war, I was simply terrified by air raids, and it was my lot to be in every one that happened in London. I tried to build up my courage by reason and prayer, etc., etc. Then one day I realized quite suddenly: As long as I try not to be afraid I shall be worse, and I shall show it one day and break. What God is asking of me, to do for suffering humanity, is to be afraid, to accept it and put up with it. Instead of kidding myself and trying to minimize the danger or to find some distraction from it, I said to myself: "For as long as this raid lasts—an hour, or eight hours— you are going to be terrified, so you must carry on and be terrified, that's all."

At once the strain ceased. Oh yes, I was terrified. But all that time I felt that God had put his hand right down through all the well upon well of darkness and horror between him and me and was holding the central point of my soul; and I knew that however afraid I was then, it would not, even could not, break me. It's only when we try not to experience our special suffering that it can really break us.

Caryll Houselander

Real peace

Real peace does not mean we suddenly are transported to a problem-free realm where nothing bad ever happens. Real peace means we can survive the chaos and confusion around us without becoming chaotic or confused.

There is no such thing as "easy peace." If you recite the Twenty-third Psalm every night before you go to sleep and really think about it, you will be soothed temporarily. But you will only be really strengthened inwardly, you will only be given real, tough, durable, inner peace, if you come to realize and recognize the firm grip of the hand of the one who is already your Shepherd!

Eugenia Price

A mother's fears

As mothers we need to be able to turn to God with our fears. Every time the children are late or lost or running a temperature of 104°, we need to be able to put our trust in someone more powerful than ourselves and say, "Please God, you love them too. Please let it be all right." If we are able to trust in God's love, it is much easier to survive these cliff-hanging worries.

Margaret Hebblethwaite

A mother's last words to her daughter

I am very, very glad when I think of you, because your whole life is given to your Savior, and I know that one day he will say to you, "Enter into the joy of thy Lord."

He does satisfy the heart of his loving, trusting child. You have found him true, I know, just as I have, and tens of thousands have. No one who gave herself wholly to him was ever disappointed at the end. No, not one.

And all the time he is with you, my child. He says to you, "Daughter, thou art ever with me and all that I have is thine." He notices everything, remembers everything, gives everything his dear child needs for life and service. She is ever with him, never, never far away from his loving heart.

If this note is ever in your hands it will be because I am out of sight, with the Lord. But I shall not be forgetting you. I do not forget you now although I see you so seldom. I shall be thinking of you, loving you, praying for you, rejoicing as I see you run your race.

God bless you and make you a blessing.

Amy Carmichael

Turn the carpet

This world which clouds thy soul with doubt
is but a carpet inside out;
as when we view these shreds and ends,
we know not what the whole intends;
so when on earth things look but odd,
they're working out some scheme of God.
What now seems random strokes will there
in order and design appear.
Then we shall praise what here we spurn'd,
for then the carpet shall be turn'd.

Hannah More

A wonderful friend

Although prison conditions were very hard, hope remained with me. I experienced no sorrow, my spirit was not depressed by fear. I was able to live through these three years with the words from St. Matthew, chapter 11, verse 30 before my eyes: "For my yoke is easy and my burden is light." Though these words from the Bible were very familiar to me before my arrest, only now do I understand how true and correct they are. Christ's burden is indeed light to bear. I experienced this in a deep way in prison many times. During my time there I had a wonderful friend, the risen Lord Jesus Christ. I experienced in prison same as did a Christian sister, who wrote from her cell that Christ gives his grace and presence to those in prison, so that one is able to endure what lies ahead. We're never alone or rejected, not even in prison.

Aida Skripnikova

I have a guardian angel

I am not afraid that I shall in any manner be defiled by the
foul infamy to which, thinking me helpless and wholly in
your grasp, you are not ashamed to condemn me. I have with
me an Angel of the Lord as a guardian of my person.
Moreover, the only Son of God, whom you know not, sur-
rounds me with an impenetrable wall; he guards me with an
ever-watchful care and is ready to ward off from me every
danger. But your gods are either made of brass—of which it
is more proper to make kettles for the use of men—or of
stones, which serve a better purpose when employed in paving
the streets. The eternal God dwells not in senseless stones, but
in the heavens; he is not confined by brass or by any other
metal, but he reigns in his glorious kingdom on high.

Attributed to Saint Agnes

Opening the door to the Spirit

"At that moment I didn't want anything except for God to take me quickly—as I was. I said, 'God, I don't know who you are. I don't know anything about you. I don't even know how to pray. Just, Lord, have your own way with me.'"

Though she did not realize it, Maude Blanford had just prayed one of the most powerful of all prayers—the prayer of relinquishment. By getting her own mind and will out of the way, she had opened the door to the Holy Spirit.

Gradually, as her knowledge of him grew, she sensed his protective love surrounding and sheltering her. Not that all pain and difficulties were over. She was still on pain-numbing drugs, still experiencing much nausea as the aftermath of the radiation.

"The will to live is terribly important," she commented. "It takes a lot of self-effort just to get out of bed, to eat again after your food has just come up. This is when too many people give up."

It took time—nine months for her bad leg to be near normal, two years for all symptoms of cancer to vanish.

Catherine Marshall LeSourd

Perfect peace

One of the disciplines of a godly woman must be the discipline of the mind. We are not free to let our emotions flip and flop all over the place. We are not free to fret and worry if we feel like it, to indulge ourselves in pouting and stewing. That doesn't mean that the blues aren't permissible; they are. Many of the Psalms are David's laying out of his feelings openly before the Lord—his "down" feelings as well as his "up" feelings.

But anxiety—that's something else. Worry is disobedience. The disciplined mind makes no room for doubting God's plans for me.

"Thou wilt keep him in perfect peace, whose mind is stayed on thee; because he trusteth in thee" (Isaiah 26:3). Life has no other soft pillow but that! All else is steep precipices and darkness and sudden new violence. But in you, Lord—in your will, in your presence—all is well.

Anne Ortlund

Balance and serenity

I have found sobriety brings balance, and balance brings serenity. In recovery, I have sometimes lost this balance, and it usually happens when I am neglecting my spiritual program. Then all the chronic symptoms—envy, resentment, self-pity, anger—of my disease reappear. Like most alcoholics, I handle anger badly, and I try to deal with this by writing out what is making me angry, and when I put it down on paper, I realize how I'm allowing it to disrupt my life. And this realization permits me to move along. I really do believe that God never gives us more than we can handle. But I also believe he expects us to do the footwork; we can't just sit back and wait for him to dump everything in our laps.

Betty Ford

God brings about the issue

Have faith in God. Faith is really believing that something good will come to pass in spite of things that are looking clean contrary. Disbelief, indifference, boredom, fear— they will come at you like swarms of gnats. Watch, from outside yourself. Go on believing in the truth. Whether the thing that baffles you (that personal relationship) looks possible or impossible is really not your question. You have your task in it, but you will be beaten in it if you let go faith in the fact that God also has his task in it. He will bring about the issue, not you.

Florence Allshorn

Be still, my soul

Be still, my soul: the Lord is on thy side;
Bear patiently the cross of grief or pain;
Leave to thy God to order and provide;
In every change he faithful will remain.
Be still, my soul: thy best, thy heavenly Friend
Through thorny ways leads to a joyful end.

Be still, my soul: thy God doth undertake
To guide the future as he has the past.
Thy hope, thy confidence let nothing shake;
All now mysterious shall be bright at last.
Be still, my soul: the waves and winds still know
His voice who ruled them while he dwelt below.

Be still, my soul: the hour is hastening on
When we shall be forever with the Lord,
When disappointment, grief, and fear are gone,
Sorrow forgot, love's purest joys restored.
Be still, my soul: when change and tears are past,
All safe and blessed we shall meet at last.

Katharina von Schlegel

On death and dying

I think a lot of old people just aren't very sensible. They only have old friends and then they live to be ninety or something, like me, and then they start moaning because their friends have gone before, as they say.

My advice to the aged woman is find some young people. Don't go to these dreadful old folks' clubs but find some young people. Put up with their casualness because it's worth it.

I don't dread dying in my sleep, but I do dread dying any other way. Mostly for the nuisance, you know. And I don't dread being dead. My heavenly Father has looked after me from the cradle and he won't stop at the grave. Through all my life he has taken care of me. Even if I just went out like a candle, what is there to dread?

An elderly widow

In death and eternal life

My mother's death was a moment of truth for me. Till then, ever since I had tried to live God's way, I had felt sure that if you did this, he kept you safe and shielded you from danger, pain, or tragedy. Now I learned that even if God does not send pain, neither does he always protect you from it. He goes through it with you, and, if you will let him, uses it for others over and over again. I also found that my faith in the eternal life, in continuing unity with those we love, was not only strengthened, but that real love for them meant that you truly let them go into God's keeping and trusted them to him. I often have the feeling that those I love are near, but I am also sure that if I demand to have that sense of their presence, I really do hold them back from the fullness of God's ongoing plan for them.

Joan Porter Buxton

# Shadows of glory

Though death walks at my heels,
and welcome,
this is the beginning,
not the end of my story.
I walk among shadows,
O Liege Lord,
my love,
Shadows
of your bright glory!

Caryll Houselander

 *Fearing death*

To fear death doesn't make me less of a Christian. It affirms my humanity. Most of us are afraid of the unknown.

I have a better chance to adjust to a new experience if I have a few clues as to what to expect. But there are very few to guide us in death. We just say to God, "I'm yours."

JoAnn Kelley Smith

No fear

I can never see why one should fear to die. When I walk into the garden here early in the morning and nearly burst with excitement at this world; and when I realize that it is only a shadow, a pale ghost of what that world must be like—then I can only feel a tremendous longing to know more of it, and to be in it.

Florence Allshorn

The leap of faith

God has not deserted me in life. Neither will he in death. And I have confidence he knows the way. I'm apprehensive and often frightened, but just as I have taken the leap of faith before, I'm prepared for this one. I believe that whatever God has in store for me, it will be better than the life I've enjoyed here—great as that has been.

Out of World War II comes the story of a father and his daughter seeking refuge from the bombs that showered London. He found a deep crater, which he thought would offer safety, and took shelter there. He called to his daughter, telling her to jump. She was afraid of the darkness below and said, "But I can't see you." And he replied, "It's all right—I can see you." So she jumped and was caught in his waiting arms. We can't see God waiting for us. But he can see us. That's the leap of faith.

JoAnn Kelley Smith

Into the hands of Infinite Love

Well, it's true we are in God's hands, and, as I meant to say, and may have said to you before, the only prayer I can say now is "Into thy hands, Father, into thy hands." And it is not only my wretched body and shivering soul that I am at last committing absolutely to the hands of Infinite Love, but, and this is so much greater a surrender, all those whom I love—above all, those whom I presumed to feel dependent on my love.

Caryll Houselander

Death of a sister

Picture her in the bosom of her beloved Spouse; this thought will soften your sorrow. Remind yourself that she is freed from the labors of this weary life and enjoys celestial happiness in company with so many other servants and friends of Jesus Christ. What a happy exchange it is to have lost her on earth in order to possess her in heaven, where she can help us far better by her intercession with the divine Majesty.

I beg of you to recommend to her your humble servant, for I have great confidence in the intercession of so holy a soul, as well as in your fervent prayers. For my part, I shall also pray for you.

Blessed Mary of the Angels

Love creates love

I know what it can feel like to part from a man whom one is in love with, for I too have done so, years and years ago. I have never had any feeling of his nearness or anything since he died, but I have always known that he is alive and that one day, I devoutly hope, we shall meet. Also, and maybe this is more important, because I loved that man I have loved many other people, animals, and things.

Caryll Houselander

Incomprehensible love

Sometimes God's love seems incomprehensible. I have two friends whose babies have died, one at ten weeks, the other at one week. Those babies who died were real persons, as their mothers knew they were. To all eternity they will exist as human persons, and yet what kind of eternity can we imagine for them? We cannot imagine. We cannot envision how God can bring to fruition in eternity the personality lost to this world. What did they achieve in this world? Only a message of the existence of love, a love whose size can be measured by the size of the pain that it leaves behind.

Margaret Hebblethwaite

Sorrow irrigates

Is it really paradoxical that when we are distressed we turn to the friend who knows what distress can be like? We don't know why, but there doesn't seem much point in going for sympathy, the deep-down, understanding kind, to those other friends whose paths have always been smooth. It is as though human beings lack a whole dimension and cannot come to maturity until they have faced sorrow. There is an old Arab proverb: "Too much sunshine makes a desert," and the human heart is very often a desert. But sorrow irrigates the desert. A few years ago a friend of mine, a poet, stricken by the death of a close friend, wrote:

Shall I complain
How swift you passed?
Could I regret the widened heart?
Could I complain of it at all?

Cicely Saunders and Mary Craig

Reach out in power and love

Suffering and death are real. I only have to pick up the papers to know that. It is there, recorded in stark words and pictures.

Suffering and death are real. I know it from my own experience, and I am afraid.

In your love and power reach out to those who suffer today, to those who mourn, those who have lost hope.

Reach out to me too, Lord, and grant me your peace.

Margaret Cundiff

Good out of evil

Hard times, and sweet

Let us so bind ourselves
that we will not only
adhere to you
in times of consolation,
in times of sweetness and devotion
and when life goes smoothly,
but yet more securely
in the bleak and bitter
seasons of the soul—
in the iron-hard winters
of the spirit.

Caryll Houselander

My purpose is to receive

A friend and I were considering life and its purpose. I said that, even with increasing paralysis and loss of speech, I believed there was a purpose for my life, but I was not sure what it was at that particular time. We agreed to pray about it for a week. I was then sure that my present purpose is simply to receive other people's prayers and kindness and to link together all those who are lovingly concerned about me, many of whom are unknown to one another.

After a while my friend said, "It must be hard to be the wounded person when, by nature, you would rather be the Good Samaritan."

It is hard. It would be unbearable were it not for my belief that the wounded person and the Samaritan are inseparable. It was the helplessness of the one that brought out the best in the other and linked them together.

I am overwhelmed by the kindness of so many Samaritans. There are those who have been praying for me for a long time and constantly reassure me of continued interest and support. There are many others who have come into my life—people I would never have met had I not been in need—who are now being asked to take care of me. I like to think that all of us have been linked together for a purpose that will prove a means of blessing to us all.

Enid Henke

Lesson in pain

I am not by nature a person who bears pain gladly or easily. Then one day God said very clearly to me, "Let go and give yourself to your pain. Stop resisting it. It is a way in which to a small degree you can enter into some understanding of my pain on the Cross." It was not easy to follow that out, but I kept on trying, and I have never forgotten that lesson. Ever since, whenever pain, whether physical or emotional, has come my way I have tried to face it in that spirit. Pain for me now is no longer an enemy to be resisted at all costs. Rather, if God allows it I can accept it as his gift, asking him to go through it with me, and then I find that invariably he uses it in some way to help or to understand the need of someone else. Obviously, I do not always succeed, but it is something to aim at and it undercuts self-pity and resentment.

Joan Porter Buxton

Real healing

What do we mean when we speak of healing? For some, it will be miraculous restoration of physical health, but for me, healing can come in many different ways. Healing can be the response by one human being to another in warmth and love and friendship. It can be doing something thoughtful or kindly. Perhaps our Lord does not always want us to receive physical healing. Certainly, in my case, I am anything but outwardly whole, yet inwardly I feel a complete person. Knowing that I have received inner health and healing, having been given a strength that can only come from God, I feel that God wants me to use my weakness to project his strength to others.

I know that my disability has given me greater compassion. It has enabled me to get alongside other human beings and share their sufferings simply because I have had a degree of suffering myself and therefore I can identify with them.

Lin Berwick

I thanked God for my experiences in the concentration camp. Now I could tell these people about my experience of the reality of Jesus Christ in the hell of Ravensbrück. The fact that I also had suffered aroused their interest, and I was entitled to speak, because I could understand them.

Corrie ten Boom

Released from fear

The word *cancer* was my secret, hidden fear, the unmention-able thing, spoken only in whispers. Yet from the moment I heard the word and knew the specialist was speaking about me, I have been released from all fears, both great and small. Because I'm a woman, because I write, because I go to lots of women's meetings as a speaker, I can talk about women's problems, I can tell about my four years of hop-ping in and out of a sick bed, major operations, radium treatment—and I can tell how I manage to cope with the commitments and give reassuring news of the progress that is being made by research.

I have so many blessings that it is impossible to count them, and I can only thank God for my sixteen wonderful years in which I have realized day by day and hour by hour the wonderful truth of God's caring power.

Josephine Hilton

A limit to self-pity

When disaster first makes its unwelcome appearance into our lives, self-pity is the first, unavoidable, normal, and probably right reaction. Courage flies out at the window, the world seems all of a sudden hostile and menacing, an alien place where we are no longer at home. We feel as though we are falling apart and are deaf to everything but the shriek of our own misery. In the early stages I don't see how it is possible to fight self-pity. We only exhaust ourselves in trying to keep it at bay. But there is a time limit, and we alone can fix it. I believe it is possible to recognize the point of no return, the moment when self-pity threatens to become malignant. And that is when we have to stand firm, for if once we allow it to get a real hold we are doomed. Self-pity is a cancer that erodes not only our courage and our will to happiness, but also our humanity and our capacity to love. It destroys us, and it destroys the friends who love us and who want to help. After all, if we come to see ourselves as the ill-used victims of outrageous fate, all our actions and thoughts will be governed by bitterness, rancor, and sour envy.

Cicely Saunders and Mary Craig

Taking stock

In the normal rush and hullabaloo of life, we have neither time nor mind for personal stocktaking. It is only when we are brought up short, when we are afraid or bewildered or disoriented, that we turn to God with an uncomprehending, frequently agnostic, cry for help. The bubble of our self-esteem has been pricked, our complacency has gone, and we are totally vulnerable. Then and only then can grace begin to operate in us, when we begin to take stock of ourselves and to listen to our inner voices.

Cicely Saunders and Mary Craig

Blessings outweigh

When I compare all my blessings with the things that are wrong, the blessings far outweigh the petty clashes and the other things. I don't know what I would do without the Lord. I've certainly been far happier the last ten years with multiple sclerosis than I ever was, healthy and strong, before I knew him.

Valerie Hadert

Counting blessings

In my opinion, the most glorious singing voice I have ever heard was the almost unbelievably beautiful contralto voice of Kathleen Ferrier. Miss Ferrier died of cancer when she was still a young woman. From her hospital bed she wrote to a close friend: "Well, here I sit in bed counting my blessings!"

Eugenia Price

Good out of all evil

Of all the feasts of the church, Holy Innocents is the most intolerable: of all sounds after the crying of children, the most terrible is the crying of Rachel weeping for her children, because they are not. Except when she is crying because they still are. I cannot reconcile the images of tiny deformed children with old men's eyes, in great pain, with what I am bound to believe of a loving, omnipotent Father. I will not assent to this pain as anything but a manifest evil.

One of the most helpful things that was ever said to me was "The definition of Almighty means that there is no evil out of which good cannot be brought." This I have found, extremely painfully, to be true.

Margaret Spufford

How great is God's love

It was on a recent Good Friday that many of our congregation became caught up in a tragedy enacted right on the threshold of the church. They had gathered on the steps to sing some of the great Passion hymns before setting off in a procession of witness to carry the cross through the streets of the city. A young man, who worked in a cafe opposite, joined them to sing with them. As they reached the last hymn, he left to go back to the cafe, where a racial brawl had broken out. In the affray he was stabbed by two white teenagers. He returned to the church steps and fell dying at the feet of the people still singing a Passion hymn. They tended for him as well as they could but were unable to save his life. He died in the ambulance on the way to the hospital.

It was many months later that a woman came to the church and introduced herself as the mother of the murdered man. She had come down from her home in Manchester to visit the place where her son had died. Then she said words that none of us who heard her will ever forget.

"I want you to know," she said, "that I have learned through this tragedy how great is God's love. There is no one a mother can love more than her son, and no loss can be greater than to see him die. But that is what God suffered for us. He saw his Son die, but he never stopped loving us. We must allow such love to fill our hearts too, not to condemn, but to save those who sin against us."

Pauline Webb

The suffering creator

On those terrible children's wards, I could neither have
worshiped nor respected any God who had not himself
cried, "My God, my God, why hast thou forsaken me?"
Because it was so, because the creator loved his creation
enough to become helpless with it and suffer in it, totally
overwhelmed by the pain of it, I found there was still hope.
But without the Garden of Gethsemane, without the tor-
ture and the gibbet, there would be no hope for any of us,
overwhelmed in the present by pain.

Margaret Spufford

Share the stories

At a women's retreat in Canada, we found that it took only a few personal stories to open the floodgates of anguish and pain. Almost everyone in the room was ready to share her struggles of faith in the face of broken marriages, broken health, broken families, broken lives. There is a deep longing to redeem the scars and amputations. Offering them as a gift to others who walk the same path is a beginning. It is precisely where we have suffered and known pain that we can be instruments of life and hope to others.

Gwen Cashmore and Joan Puls

The people we need

I am so much a sinner that I understand well how the
slightest discouragement from outside oneself, added to
the chronic close-on-despair inside, can crush one altogether.
One doesn't want a preacher, or even a shining example, but
someone who will share the burden, even if they know they
can't carry their own.

Caryll Houselander

Affirm me

I need to know that God has not abandoned me, but accepts me with all my human weakness, my questions, my fears, my doubts, my ambivalence, and my contradictions.

I need the affirmation of my humanity that Rita gave me when she entered my hospital room and through my tears assured me, "Don't be afraid—don't feel bad about crying—our Lord didn't want to die and he cried the night through. Even on the cross he felt the loneliness and the separation—just try to be a person—don't try to be an angel."

JoAnn Kelley Smith

Don't give up on me

Lord,
I so soon get thrown by circumstances.
I panic over little things,
faith goes out the window.
Be patient with me.
Remind me of all the way you have brought me,
provided for me.
Feed me with your living word
that I may grow in understanding,
in trust and love.
Don't give up on me, will you?
—But I know you won't,
because you promised you wouldn't,
and you always keep your promises.

Margaret Cundiff

A happy Christ

What you have helped me to see is a very happy Christ. I can't get away from that. He's not saying, "Be like this and you'll be good." He's saying, "Be like this and you'll be happy, and it's the only way of happiness." It's not how other people affect you, it's how you affect other people that matters all the time. Give and give and give happiness, and you'll get it all the time. That's the way God has made things work, and this stupid me, wanting to get away from the pain of this place, sees now and then that that wouldn't make me happy. It's accepting it that makes me happy, and I have been very happy lately, since I have seen the happy Christ.

Florence Allshorn

PART THREE

The Real World

Women of vision are women of today—juggling busy lives, keeping homes together, and seeing that elderly parents and rebellious teenagers and grubby toddlers are fed and cared for. And yet we are not hermetically sealed off from the "big issues." In this section you'll find material from women imprisoned for living out their faith—and you'll hear some clarion calls to a new vision.

Our daily work

Spend it wisely

Time is like loose change. It is given to us here below to buy the real things of eternity. Let us use it!

Saint Julie Billiart

Start where we are

In the present world of turmoil, what can we do?

I think constantly of a saying of Luther's which, roughly translated, runs: "Even if the world came to an end tomorrow, we will still, in spite of that, plant our little apple tree today!"

We can all start with our own hearts, our own homes, making, if we can, a little pool of peace where others may find refreshment. We can pray, regularly and hopefully. We can keep our tempers, do the small household chores cheerfully, help our neighbors, stop grumbling! Very, very insignificant things in the face of world problems, but as the old saying goes, we can put a drop of oil on the troubled waters; and each of us may serve God's purpose as far as we may.

Elizabeth Fox Howard

Real Christian work

In nothing has the church so lost her hold on reality as in her failure to understand and respect the secular vocation. She has allowed work and religion to become separate departments and is astonished to find that, as a result, the secular work of the world is turned to purely selfish and destructive ends, and the greater part of the world's intelligent workers have become irreligious, or at least, uninterested in religion. But is it astonishing? How can anyone remain interested in a religion which seems to have no concern with nine-tenths of life? The church's approach to an intelligent carpenter is usually confined to exhorting him not to be drunk and disorderly in his leisure hours, and to come to church on Sunday. What the church should be telling him is that he should make good tables. Church by all means, and decent forms of amusement, certainly—but what use is all that if in the very center of his life and occupation he is insulting God with bad carpentry? No crooked table legs or ill-fitting drawers ever, I dare swear, came out of the carpenter's shop at Nazareth. Nor, if they did, could anyone believe that they were made by the same hand that made heaven and earth.

Let the church remember this: that every maker and worker is called to serve God in his profession or trade— not outside it. . . . The official church wastes time and energy, and, moreover, commits sacrilege, in demanding that secular workers should neglect their proper vocation in order to do Christian work—by which she means ecclesiastical work. The only Christian work is good work well done. Let the church see to it that the workers are Christian people and do their work well, as to God: then all work will be Christian work, whether it is church embroidery or sewage farming.

Dorothy L. Sayers

Drop by drop

It may be a drop in the ocean, but the ocean is made up of drops.

Mother Teresa of Calcutta

Today

You see, God's will for you is to serve him, in his way, as he chooses now. It is only a want of humility to think of extreme vocations, like being a nun or a nurse, while you try to bypass your present obvious vocation. Today you have to use what you have today, and do not look beyond it.

Caryll Houselander

The imprint of Jesus

God must take first place in my life. That is clear in the commandments given by God and confirmed by the words of Jesus, and I am required to show that in my life—by what I do, what I say, how I think, my attitude to other people, every aspect of life. It must show as clearly in my life as the imprint of a coin.

What do others see as I stand beside them at the supermarket checkout, in the bus line, as we exchange greetings in the street? What about the conversations I have, the way I use my money and time, my response to people and situations in my own community? Have I dulled the image of Jesus Christ? Overlaid it with grime and muck, allowed it to be tarnished?

Margaret Cundiff

Into all the world

Until we make our religion a part of our common life,
until we bring Christianity from its retreat to live in the
world and dwell among men; until we have brought it from
the closet to the active scene, from the church to the world,
whether that world be the court, the senate, the exchange,
the public office, the private counting-house, the courts of
justice, the professional departments, or the domestic
drawing room, it will not have fully accomplished what it
was sent on earth to do.

Hannah More

Advice for women in the world

Dear Children: As to your dressing, I can't believe that there should be any neglect of that beauty God has given you, soe it be done with this caution. As to your conversation, there is nothing forbidden butt what is either prophane, or unjust. 'Tis true, wee should not preach in the Withdrawing roome, butt wee must, by our lookes shew that wee fear God, and that wee dare not hear anything filthy, or that tends to the prejudice of our Neighbor; wee may divert people, and be innocently merry; butt then wee must not please our selves in the thoughts of it. As to your retirement, if you have been faulty, read some Chapter that doe most divinely sett forth the Love of God to us, that your sorrow for sin may proceed from the sense you have of God's great mercy and love and not from fear of Hell which terrifyes and damnation amazes, and I am never the better for those reflections.

Margaret Blagge

A blessing

What you hold, may you always hold.
What you do, may you always do and never abandon.
But with swift pace, light step,
and unswerving feet,
so that even your steps stir up no dust,
go forward
securely, joyfully, and swiftly,
on the path of prudent happiness,
believing nothing,
agreeing with nothing
which would dissuade you from this resolution
or which would place a stumbling block for you on the way,
so that you may offer your vows to the Most High
in the pursuit of that perfection
to which the Spirit of the Lord has called you.

Saint Clare of Assisi

Women's work

No person will deny the importance attached to the character and conduct of a woman, in all her domestic and social relations, when she is filling the station of a daughter, a wife, a mother, or a mistress of a family. But it is a dangerous error to suppose that the duties of females end here. Their gentleness, their natural sympathy with the afflicted, their quickness of discernment, their openness to religious impressions are points of character (not unusually to be found in our sex) which evidently qualify them, within their own peculiar province, for a far more extensive field of usefulness.

I rejoice to see the day in which so many women of every rank, instead of spending their time in trifling and unprofitable pursuits, are engaged in works of usefulness and charity. Earnestly is it to be desired that the number of these valuable laborers in the cause of virtue and humanity may be increased, and that all of us may be made sensible of the infinite importance of redeeming the time, of turning our talents to account, and of becoming the faithful, humble, devoted followers of a crucified Lord, who went about *doing good.*

Elizabeth Fry

Faith and life

Those who are interested in reading about having babies
do not expect to turn the page and find themselves up
against a lot of holy talk. Those who are interested in
reading about God do not expect to have to wade through
a heap of dirty diapers to get there. But to keep life and
religion apart in such a way is false to both sides. More
and more persistently, theologians throughout the world
are calling for an experience-based theology. They know
that if faith does not spring out of and return to the
ground soil of daily existence, then it means nothing. Faith
needs life to find its true nature.

At the same time life needs faith. The strong emotions
aroused by motherhood and the everyday slog of bringing
up children find their true meaning as part of a relationship with God.

Margaret Hebblethwaite

The results are not important

You say to me, "There are so few who really profit by all our work." I say to you, "It does not matter!" Let us go on sowing the seed just the same. Give of your best even if only a very few profit. It would be satisfying to see results, but it is not results that are important. Let us do what we can and God will do the rest.

Saint Julie Billiart

Reverence for things

The relation between us and *things* is not to be despised. They are entitled to a measure of reverence not only because of their origin, but because they may at any moment be used by God to speak to us. Perhaps we miss urgent messages by ignoring the sacramental language of the everyday world. Perhaps we are not only depriving ourselves, but also failing to put into the material world the spiritual content it needs. It is not only nature, the creation, which in Paul's words is waiting for the revealing of the sons of God; this whole complex worldwide network of twentieth-century civilization is waiting to be blessed by those whose minds are "set to hallow all they find."

Mary F. Smith

Sweeping statement

In the same chapter as we read about the Good Shepherd, we also read that God is like a woman sweeping for a lost coin. I know nothing about sheep, and a lot about sweeping, but I've never yet seen a woman sweeping, in a stained glass window.

Lois Wilson

Gift and work

I recently read an old German saying, "The gift becomes the work." I wanted to protest: *no, unfair*. But then I recalled a conversation with an aspiring writer. He had a great idea for a play, but he just hadn't been able to get anything down on paper. He asked if I thought it would be helpful if he got a group of people together to flesh out the idea.

"Well, yes—maybe. It might give you some clarity. But ultimately a committee isn't going to write your play. Someday you'll have to sit down and stare at an empty page or screen and fill it with words." Like the Rich Young Ruler, this man's face fell. It wasn't what he wanted to hear. He wanted a gift. He was willing to organize a support group, but the gift itself would require a personal struggle he didn't want to face.

Think of Mary. The gift of a child—even the unique child Jesus—required twenty years of motherly chores: serving meals, weaving cloth, laundering swaddling rags and then tunics.

In a mysterious way, God's gift to us becomes our work for God, even as God works in us.

Evelyn Bence

Prayer and the cook

[The Lord said:] "I have not merely chosen her to serve me for an hour in the day, but that she may be continually with me—that is, that she may perform all her actions for my glory, and with the same intention with which she would desire to pray. Let her also practice this devotion in all the trouble which she finds in her employment—namely, to have a constant desire that all those who benefit by her labor may not only find bodily refreshment, but that they may be incited to love me interiorly and be strengthened in all good; and each time that she acts thus, her labors and works will be to me as if she presented me with so many different victuals."

Saint Gertrude the Great

The imperfect boss

[The Lord:] "Do you not know that not only this person, but all those who have charge of this my beloved community have some defects, since no one can be entirely free from them in this life? It is far more virtuous to submit to a person whose faults are apparent, than to one who always appears perfect."

[Gertrude:] "Although I am full of joy at perceiving great merit in inferiors, I ardently desire that superiors should be free from faults."

[The Lord:] "I, who know all their weaknesses, sometimes permit them, in the diversity of their employments, to be sullied by some stain, because otherwise they might never attain so high a degree of humility. Therefore, as the merit of inferiors is increased both by the perfections and imperfections of their superiors, so the merit of superiors increases by the perfections and imperfections of inferiors, even as the different members of the same body contribute to mutual increase."

Saint Gertrude the Great

Justice for all

 Open

I stand.
I open myself to God.
I kneel.
I listen.
I step into God's presence.
I float in the encompassing ocean of God's love
like a sieve in the sea.
I breathe in and out:
breathing in the mercy of God,
breathing out the pain of my sadness.
I am still
at rest with God,
who is deep within me
and all around me.
Out of that deep center
I weave a prayer
of God's presence,

affirming that God is,
that God is with the poor,
that God is with the outcast,
that God is with me.
I call upon God's Spirit.
She rests like a butterfly
shimmering on a branch.
She confronts the hurt,
which lies curled
at the heart of society.
She leads me out,
from active prayer,
into prayerful action.

Kate McIlhagga

Individuals wanted

Well-known musicians, painters, and writers live on in the
lives of millions of future generations who enjoy the gifts
they have created. The valuable legacy they leave to the
world is not of riches but in how they used their great
artistic gifts. Yet all of us have been endowed with some
gift which we can use to benefit humanity. I have always
been surprised by the number of well-meaning people with
a genuine desire to help who have looked at the enormity
facing humanity and said, "The problem is too big—there
is nothing I, as an individual, can do to help." The truth is
that there are few problems confronting humanity that are
incapable of solution if only a sufficient number of human
beings apply their hearts and energies.

Sue Ryder

Turning the world upside down

Whoever started the rumor that Christianity is not a political faith got the wrong end of the stick. It is not only political, it is revolutionary, for it seeks to turn the world upside down and ensure that those who are now last—the poor, the sick, homeless, and oppressed—will be first. A Christian will not be other-worldly; he or she will look for God in the challenge that God is presenting us with in this world.

Elizabeth Stuart

Thy kingdom come

The life of the planet, and especially its human life, is a life in which something has gone wrong, and badly wrong. Every time that we see an unhappy face, an unhealthy body, hear a bitter or despairing word, we are reminded of that. The occasional flashes of pure beauty, pure goodness, pure love, which show us what God wants and what he is, only throw into more vivid relief the horror of cruelty, greed, oppression, hatred, ugliness, and also the mere muddle and stupidity which frustrate and bring suffering into life. Unless we put on blinkers, we can hardly avoid seeing all this; and unless we are warmly wrapped up in our own cozy ideas and absorbed in our own interests, we surely cannot help feeling the sense of obligation, the shame of acquiescence, the call to do something about it. To say day by day "Thy Kingdom come"—if these tremendous words really stand for a conviction and desire—does not mean "I quite hope that some day the Kingdom of God will be established, and peace and goodwill prevail. But at present I don't see how it is to be managed or what I can do about it." On the contrary, it means, or should mean, "Here am I! Send me!"—active, costly collaboration with the Spirit in whom we believe.

Evelyn Underhill

Will he find faith on earth?

Who among us has the courage to ask in our assemblies
and our meeting rooms the hard question: When the Son
of man comes, will he find any faith on earth? (Luke 18:8)
For are not the implications meant for us, who plan pro-
grams to address poverty and injustice, and regularly claim
our high salaries and pursue our comfortable lifestyles? For
us, who preach sacrifice and generosity to our parishioners,
and sport our latest-model Oldsmobiles and expensive golf
clubs? For us, who profess solidarity with the poor and
continue to build retirement homes and travel in style and
dress like our secular counterparts? For us, who read the
Scriptures, while we shun the Samaritans of our day, live in
discord, compete for positions, and shirk confrontation
with those who perpetrate injustice? The word of the Lord
to us is a call to repentance, to open our lives to conversion, and to allow the Scriptures to judge and rebuke us.

Joan Puls

Caring for the poor

Young ladies should be accustomed to set apart a fixed part of their time, as sacred to the poor, whether in relieving, instructing, or working for them; and the performance of this duty must not be left to the event of contingent circumstances, or the operation of accidental impressions, but it must be established into a principle and wrought into a habit. A specific portion of the day must be allotted to it, on which no common engagement must be allowed to entrench.

Hannah More

An example of service

In my ninth year, my dear mother took me to London Yearly Meeting, and there for the first time I had the privilege of listening to that eminent servant of the Lord, Elizabeth Fry. I shall never forget the impression she made upon my young mind by her sweet voice, beautiful face, and her earnest pleading as she spoke of the prisoners, the suffering, and the outcast. I was too young to understand one half of what she said, yet good seed was sowed then and there which led to active labor in after years. In the solemn silence that followed after she took her seat, my childish heart was lifted in the prayer that I might grow as good as she was, and work in the same way.

Elizabeth L. Comstock

Nothing is too small for God

I expressed to my mother a fear that God would not care for a little child like me. She replied by lifting me up to see a bird's nest in the hedgerow and explaining to me that God taught the little bird to build its nest and to rear its young; and then bade me pluck a little flower at my feet, and pointed out how nothing was so small to escape his notice.

Elizabeth L. Comstock

Giving from a distance

Some people are only too willing to give from a distance—
to have sickness and misery kept out of sight, decontami-
nated. Their unexamined motive is not to heal suffering but
to disinfect it.

Caryll Houselander

The gospel of peace

The experience of sharing the lives of the poor in my community in Africa shook me out of my complacency and insensitivity to injustice happening all around me at home. On my return to England, my eyes were opened for the first time. I saw men and women who had no homes lining up for soup at day centers, while in the streets, people walking aimlessly with blank, lifeless expressions on their faces are those whose self-esteem and purpose in life has been eroded by long-term unemployment.

Yet at the same time the government in my name spends billions of pounds on weapons systems intending to destroy millions of people—each person created by the God who created me. I ask myself over again, "How can I have been oblivious to the stockpiling of nuclear weapons in this country? How can I all these years have failed to grasp the point of Christ's Gospel of Peace?"

Margaret Holden

Solidarity with the poor

It is tempting for us to rush into singing the songs of the oppressed as if we could indeed quite simply make their words our own. We should feel uneasy with a lusty singing of the triumph songs of the poor, when we have no right to triumphalism, given where we are standing and whose side we are in fact on. To pretend that we are the poor may give us the feeling of occupying the high moral ground we naively assume is theirs, but it doesn't assist either worship or action because it is untruthful.

Much harder, but in the end more hopeful, is to seek solidarity with the poor. Solidarity means truthfully recognizing the place we stand in, while really seeing theirs; and then, with love and honesty and commitment, exploring the connections between us and working together for change. For us, it will mean facing the complexity and ambivalence of where we are placed, as Christians living in the rich world who want to pray in solidarity with the poor. It will entail acknowledging both our participation in sin and our own woundedness. It will require repentance (a change of stance in relation to the evil that seeks to surround us). But it will also release us to share in a passionate desire for change in the structures of the world—for our sake too. We will recognize a struggle and find joy, forgiveness, and salvation as we join it.

Janet Morley

Great joy among the poor

I talked with catechists and priests in refugee camps and slums, with a Lutheran bishop and a Jesuit professor, with mothers and wives of the missing—talked about the suffering servant of God while talking about the poor. They spoke from an inner power which the Bible calls the "strength in weakness," the "hope against hope," the "great joy among the poor." I must confess that I did not fully understand and that I often resist this with the rational, economic, and psychological tools with which my culture has equipped me.

What I understand is that there is a spirituality which does not permit us to define life through money and power, a spirit of courage, strength, and joy which does not submit to this central definition of our culture—money and might. What I do not understand is where the joy comes from, the struggle and the solidarity, or the certainty of the poor that God is with them. What I do not understand is the mystery of God; it is the fire which I, a doubting woman in Europe overwhelmed by the shadows, often think can be extinguished.

Dorothee Soelle

The gift of liberation

The theology of liberation is one of the great gifts of the
poor of Latin America to Christianity, as well as to the middle class of the rich world, to which I belong. It is a gift which
is not used up; it nourishes me, as it nourishes the poor.

"And the bush was blazing, yet it was not consumed."
This is how I experience the pictures, the prayers, the biblical interpretation, the belief of this theology. It represents
a gift to the world church, even if the latter has not yet
grasped it.

The various forms of Christianity—orthodoxy, liberal-
ism, and liberation theology—are still wrestling with one
another. But we can recognize the signs of liberation: the
blind begin to see, the lame begin to walk, and the poor are
given back their dignity. The God of the poor appears, and
in this epiphany of God the Christian religion unfolds its
revolutionary strength. This religion is alive in the new
social movements for peace, justice, and the integrity of
creation.

Dorothee Soelle

The poor are our teachers

The poor are the teachers, according to a basic principle of liberation theology. What do they teach me then, when the gap between my technology, knowledge, money, and power and theirs is unbridgeable? How have they then "evangelized" me, how have they converted me, what have they given me?

From the poor of Latin America I learn their hope, their toughness, their anger, and their patience. I learn a better theology in which God is not Lord-over-us but Strength-in-us. In which the miracles of Jesus are not distinguished from ours; we too drive out demons and heal the sick. I learn trust in the people of God. I overcome skepticism, false conciliatoriness, and short-sighted illusory hopes. I practice betrayal of my own class. I leave their spiritual apartheid and move toward the liberation of all. I gain a part; I belong to them. I am less alone. I begin to hunger and thirst after righteousness. I am evangelized, and I sing along from the new person:

Creadores de la historia,
constructores de nueva humanidad.

Dorothee Soelle

The power of love

Real power

Spiritual power is the power to influence others through one's own being—by example, by kindness, by wisdom, by love, and above all through prayer. Institutional power has to do with ambition and control; spiritual power has much to do with surrendering control.

Penny Jamieson

How we love one another

We have become excellent social servants, Christian organizers, doctors, nurses, teachers, but we have lost the essential spring of "fellowship one with another." People outside Christianity look at our little Christian groups, our parish churches, our Christian schools, colleges, societies, and fail to see them shining out like light in dark places. Christian committees, diocesan councils, missionary bodies—all these should be centers of light, of the Spirit, and so often they are not. Instead of "How these Christians love one another," we hear "I never go near church societies or parish organizations, there is so much gossip and rivalry." The criticism would not matter if it were not so often the truth.

Florence Allshorn

Christian love

My very soul is sick of religious controversy. Christianity is a broad basis. Bible Christianity is what I love. [It] does not insist on opinions indifferent in themselves; [it is] a Christianity practical and pure, which teaches holiness, humility, repentance, and faith in Christ; and which after summing up all the evangelical graces, declares that the greatest of these is charity.

Hannah More

Do not ask . . .

Do not ask "What can I do?" but "What can God not do?"

Corrie ten Boom

The servant

Once, some time ago, God brought to my mind the phrase, "Jesus is among you as him that serveth." He was teaching me to be a servant, and he gave me all sorts of boring servant things to do for a few particularly bossy people, in trying circumstances. One day I got utterly fed up. "Lord," I said, "I just hate being a servant. I much prefer it when somebody else waits on me than when I wait on somebody else. I do it because you say so, and because you were a servant, and you want your disciples to be servants. But why? What's so special about being a servant? Couldn't you have invented something more fun for your disciples to be?"

Then he answered, something like this: "If I came to you as a King of kings and Lord of lords, you'd be frightened. And if I came to you as one in authority, many people have hang-ups about those in authority and would refuse to listen. And if I came to you as your equal, many people have rivalry situations with their equals and would refuse to listen. But nobody is threatened by a servant. A servant is someone you order about. You can send him out of the room if you like; you needn't listen to him. He does jobs for you. I am your servant because I love you, and out of my love for you I make myself available as your servant, so as not to frighten you off and so that people may be won to my love. That is why I want my disciples to be servants."

Sylvia Mary Alison

Only channels

When Jesus tells us to love our enemies, he himself will give us the love with which to do it. We are neither factories nor reservoirs of his love, only channels. When we understand that, all excuse for pride is eliminated.

Corrie ten Boom

Love like Jesus

We knew well enough in theory that the love that Jesus Christ had said was to be like his own does not start like that, that it does not start with the romantic love of the poets but with the very unpoetical neighbor. There was a difference between the thing we had known as friendship and this all-embracing friendliness which Christ epitomized in his own life.

Florence Allshorn

We do not love

That we love is one of the illusions we moderns most cherish about ourselves. We will admit cheerfully that we are not "strictly" truthful, that we are lazy, greedy, self-indulgent, proud, angry (though we prefer to say righteously indignant), that we take the Lord's name in vain and profane the Sabbath, but all these minor sins, we imply, are amply compensated for by the way we love. "I love people," we say frequently, complacently, and as conventionally as the pious used to boast that they were saved by grace.

Yet obviously we do not love, or the world would not be what it is today. We do not love vividly enough even to avoid conflicts among those who seriously wish to get along together and accomplish good works. When we encounter people of opposing politics, different races, or economic theories, when we meet with opponents who quite openly do not care whether they reach agreement or not so long as they get what they want, our bankruptcy of love proclaims itself in the feuds, persecutions, discriminations, wars, and chaos of our times.

Elizabeth Gray Vining

Children—the real VIPs

Thank God for those who have taken seriously to heart the command of Jesus to care for little ones. Thank God for their faithfulness and love. Do we, though, see the care of children as a priority in our church or community? Do we do anything for them personally? I know how difficult it is to get people to teach in Sunday school, run youth clubs, even give a hand in the nursery. I hear the grumbles of good Christian people when a child cries during a service, or when a couple of toddlers decide to go and play games in the aisle. I know my own feelings when the noise level goes above what I consider acceptable. I get edgy and selfishly wish the parents would take them out.

Yet my greatest joys have been when those same little folk have been brought up for a blessing, when they so trustingly run up to me; and I am thankful to them for giving me another chance. These are the real VIPs. They have so much to teach me about love and acceptance, about forgiveness and the joy of living each moment to the full.

Margaret Cundiff

Strong enough love

It seems to me that what matters is to create in this world a force of love strong enough to combat that of hate—and more particularly of fear. The official hate propaganda is one of the greatest tragedies of war. And there ought to be a continual quiet resistance of it. There is not room for love and hate in one heart.

Caryll Houselander

The way of self or the way of love

Some of us were good at taking prayers, others at talking in study groups, others at practical work, but it was in none of these things as such, it was in the actual attitude and deed over a saucepan, or in your quality of thinking of someone else, whether you took sides or healed the separation between sides that was the actual test. You can sit in your principal's room, or before your class, and talk with real earnestness, but the great things are not won like that. Humility, generosity, peacemaking only rise from the actually controlled deed, the love-restrained reaction, the detached-from-self sight of truth in a situation in which the truth is not pleasant for you. In the actual working together you have to change your natural self-guarding laziness and carelessness if you are to live at peace. The adventures are endless and it is a continual actual choosing whether you go the way of self or the way of love. You cannot cover over what you are by any amount of brilliant talk, even spiritual talk. We could talk in the chapel without the guilt of hypocrisy only as we lived in the house.

Florence Allshorn

Much and warm loving

The true proficiency of the soul consists not so much in deep thinking, or eloquent speaking, or beautiful writing, as in much and warm loving. Now, if you ask me in what way this much and warm love may be acquired, I answer: By resolving to do the will of God, and by watching to do his will as often as occasion offers. Those who truly love God love all good wherever they find it. They seek all good to all people. They commend all good, they always acknowledge and defend all good. They have no quarrels. They bear no envy. O Lord, give me more and more of this blessed love! It will be a magnificent comfort in the hour of death to know that we are on our way to be judged by him whom we have loved above all things. We are not going to a strange country, since it is his country whom we love and who loves us.

Saint Teresa of Ávila

Lessons in charity

Your devotedness throughout my illness, dear reverend Mother, has also taught me many a lesson of charity. No remedy seems too costly, and should one fail, you try something else. When I am present at recreation, what precautions you take to protect me from the slightest draft! All this makes me feel that I ought to be as compassionate for the spiritual infirmities of my sisters as you are, Mother, for my bodily ills.

Saint Thérèse of Lisieux

To a friar claiming his love better than hers

If I believed that your habit would add one spark to my
love, I would not hesitate to tear it from you, if I could
obtain it in no other way. Whatever you merit more than I,
through the renunciation you have made for God's sake and
through your religious life, which continually enables you
to merit, I do not seek to obtain—these are yours—but
that I cannot love God as much as yourself, you can never
make me believe.

[Subsequent prayer:] O Love, who shall prevent me
from loving you? Not only in the world, married as I am,
but even if I should find myself in a camp of soldiers, I
could not be prevented from loving you. If the world or if
the husband could impede love, what would such love be
but a thing of feeble virtue and mean capacity? As for me, I
know by what I have experienced that divine love can be
conquered or impeded by nothing. It conquers all things.

Saint Catherine of Genoa

Why we love

The reason why God's servants love creatures so much is that they see how much Christ loves them, and it is one of the properties of love to love what is loved by the persons we love.

Saint Catherine of Siena

Head and heart

Let each one give us the benefit of her intelligence today.
No one has too much.

No one can have too much heart. If only the intention
is pure we should love every creature on this earth.

Saint Teresa of Ávila

Life together

Only one course

The church's struggle is to stand [by] the way of truth and follow the Lord straightforwardly, regardless of everything else. When the church is fighting, I can't remain uninvolved. One can be a militant atheist or a nonmilitant atheist, one can be simply a nonbeliever, indifferent toward both faith and atheism, but for the Christian there is only one course. The Christian can't be anything but militant. Once you know the truth, this means following it, upholding it, and if necessary, suffering for it. I can't be different. I can't act differently.

Aida Skripnikova

Ships in the night

The world is faced with bad news, and yet there is a great Christian church which is reputed to be the custodian of good news; there is the church's awakened evangelistic concern, and the world's bewildered groping for the light, and yet they seem to pass each other in the dark.

Florence Allshorn

Keeping on

Wherever we are there are small situations going wrong, and we are to redeem them, but if we start on the way of redemption and refuse when it begins to make us suffer, whether it is our pride, or our nerves, or our comfort, we are most horribly disloyal.

Florence Allshorn

Careful with that plumb line!

If you feel strong and correct, look out! If you go about trying to set others straight according to your plumb line, God help you! And God help the others you are trying to "help."

One woman wrote, "My mother is a marvelous woman, but she is right about everything! I love her, but I simply can't live in the house with her and neither can my sister."

Only God is right about everything. Only God's plumb line falls straight, and only God has a right to use it.

Eugenia Price

I give you

Lord Jesus:
I give you my hands, to do your work.
I give you my feet, to go your way.
I give you my eyes, to see as you do.
I give you my tongue, to speak your words.
I give you my mind, that you may think in me.
I give you my spirit, that you may pray in me.
Above all, I give you my heart,
that you may love in me your Father and all mankind.
I give you my whole self, that you may grow in me.
So that it is you, Lord Jesu,
Who lives and works and prays in me.

The Grail Society

A gift from God

"Love and do what you will," said St. Augustine, but he did not mean, as we seem to interpret it, to pretend to love and be as bad as you want to be. He meant, if you really love, you cannot do ill; all the things that you wish to do, informed by your love, will be beneficent.

Love—powerful, healing, quickening, enduring, the bond of peace and of all virtues—is of God. We cannot constrain it of our own effort, but we can have it as a gift from him, if we want it enough, if we pray for it urgently, unceasingly. Pour it into our hearts in a generous, life-giving flood, for we have sore need of it.

Elizabeth Gray Vining

Go deep

What was Jesus saying when he told the fishermen to go deeper before they let down their nets?

Perhaps that relying on shallow, surface resources will not be enough for authentic living, and that—within a discipline of stillness and trust—we must let down our defenses and delve deep into the resources of God. Then we might be able to chance the impossible.

Perhaps, too, he was saying that there are no quick fixes in the missionary enterprise, that we must enter deeply into the lives—the joys, wounds, fears, and dreams—of people, in order to be Christ to them in their situation. A redemptive involvement with one another is a deep and self-sacrificial involvement.

Thus his words have implications for both prayer and action. When we "pray deep," we will be able to "live deep."

Kate Compston

You too can be a survivor

Sometimes I'm asked if I feel I have a mission. I don't. I'm not that presumptuous. I don't think God looked down and said, "Here's Betty; we're going to use her to sober up alcoholics." But I do think people relate to someone who has the same problems they have and who overcomes them. And I think God has allowed me—along with thousands of others—to carry a message that says, there's help out there, and you too can be a survivor. Look at us. Look at me.

Betty Ford

Harvest festival

We offer to you,
Swordless Lord,
those who have perished
by the sword.
We offer our harvest festival,
the barren earth,
the yield of blood,
sown in the potter's field.
At least, not a lie
in your presence, Lord.
We offer ourselves
and the waste of our conquering,
we who have lived and died
by the sword.

Caryll Houselander, written August 10, 1945

Special Sunday

One of the great sadnesses I personally feel is the loss of Sunday. It has been gradually eroded away until we are left with a day like any other day of the week when people rush frantically around, getting nowhere fast. A backlash against the Victorian Sunday, maybe, but the God-given gift of a day of rest was intended for our good—body, mind, and spirit. The human frame cannot go on day after day, week after week, without regular breaks, a release from work and routine. The mind cannot continue to cope with the burdens we place on it, while the spiritual side shrivels, dies, and the wholeness of life that God intended for us is put out of joint, and deformed, and we all suffer. I look forward to Sunday. It is for me a heaven-sent opportunity to share with others, to have time to spend in God's house and with his people, to be free from the demands of the week, to be able to relax, to breathe, to be.

Margaret Cundiff

What good is freedom?

I'm not a heroine. I love freedom and would very much like to be free now with my family and friends. But I can't buy freedom at any price; I don't want to act against my conscience. I love freedom, but what good is freedom to me if I can't call God my Father? The knowledge that my soul and thoughts are free encourages and strengthens me.

Aida Skripnikova

Messengers

It suddenly strikes me
with overwhelming force:
It was women
who were first to spread the message of Easter—
the unheard of!
It was women
who rushed to the disciples,
who, breathless and bewildered,
passed on the greatest message of all:
He is alive!
Think if women had kept silence
in the churches!

Marta Wilhelmsson

Christ for the world

When I saw and laughed at the oversized American pants sent as relief goods, I realized that I, too, might be doing the same thing: bringing an "oversized unfit" Jesus in the Immaculate Host to an uncomprehending people. Not that I don't appreciate Jesus in the Eucharist, but that having focused perhaps too much attention on the Host, I failed to encounter him alive in the [Bukidnon]. After all, did I bring Jesus there, or was he not there already, waiting for me?

A Sister from Bukidnon

Married or unmarried

I don't think it makes any difference whether you are married or unmarried. Whether you are married or unmarried is a circumstance within the Christian life. If you are married, you have a special task; if you are unmarried, you have something else to do. Both have a different witness to give. I think the married home can be one of the greatest witnesses you can make these days, because there are so many unhappy marriages, so much misery. In being married you can redeem the word *marriage* and make it something beautiful again. On the other hand, I think the unmarried person has something very fine to do, in showing that without having anything the world says you must have if you are going to be happy, you can still be happy and fulfilled, and I am very glad I have been able to prove that true. I had no parents since the age of three. I never had any money, never had any future, I tried to be an artist and couldn't, I never had a husband or children, yet I am as happy as anybody I know. I am really fulfilled. So I do not think it matters.

Florence Allshorn

Family or household?

In New Testament times, the household existed in Hebrew, Greek, and Roman societies as a voluntary association of parents, children, servants, and other dependents for their mutual benefit. It is not surprising that the household played an important role in the growth and stability of the first churches. Whereas the household can be composed of misfits and outcasts, the family—whether nuclear or extended—excludes people who do not belong. Thus the popular concept of the local church as a family is based on its exclusiveness. It is time for western Christians to abandon the idolatry of the family and to explore the implications of the biblical metaphors of the Household of God and the Household of Faith.

Marion Beales

Changes

If we are really, and always, and equally ready to do whatso-
ever the King appoints, all the trials and vexations arising
from any change in his appointments simply do not exist.
If he appoints me to work there, shall I lament that I am
not to work here? If he appoints me to wait indoors today,
am I to be annoyed because I am not to work out-of-
doors? If I meant to *write* his messages this morning, shall
I grumble because he sends interrupting visitors, rich or
poor, to whom I am to *speak* them, or "show kindness" for
his sake, or at least obey his command, "Be courteous"? If
all my members are really at his disposal, why should I be
put out if today's appointment is some simple work for my
hands or errands for my feet, instead of some seemingly
more important doing of head or tongue?

Frances Ridley Havergal

Follow the light

The eternal mysteries come into time for us individually under widely differing forms. The tiny child mothers its doll, croons to it, spends herself upon it, why she cannot tell you; and we who are here in our extreme youth, never to be men and women grown in this world, nurse our ideal, exchange it, refashion it, call it by many names; and at last in here or hereafter we find in its naked truth the Child in the manger, even as the Wise Men found him when they came from the East to seek a great King. There is but one necessary condition of this finding; we must follow the particular manifestation of light given us, never resting until it rests—over the place of the Child. And there is but one insurmountable hindrance, the extinction of or drawing back from the light truly apprehended by us. We forget this, and judge others by the light of our own soul.

Margaret Fairless Barber

How to negotiate

I have made an important discovery: One must never tell
people that they are unreasonable, as if they themselves
were blind to the fact. This is to be *too blunt*; self-love is
mounted guard at the door and no one passes that sentinel.
It is wiser to make a legitimate feint and creep in by some
narrow passage, making oneself as small as possible. No
one pays any attention to you, and in this way, one pene-
trates into the heart of the citadel. Once there, one can
cleverly awaken certain good thoughts which slumber in a
corner of the conscience or the judgment; this thought has
but to manifest itself and its proprietor is reminded that,
after all, if he were not so weak and if it were not for this
or that, or for such and such a thing, he would much prefer
to follow the path of common sense than to feel that he is
positively turning his back on it. This done, the first point
is gained, for the eyes are now open to the light without
seeing who holds the torch, and none ever appeal from the
tribunal of their own judgment.

Lucie Christine

Good judgment

To avoid mistaken judgments, we should cultivate our powers of observation. There is a vast difference between merely looking at a thing and really seeing it. Then we take many things for granted that should be tested and tried. Our own minds would rather that someone else would do the thinking and we unthinkingly follow. It is well sometimes to get away from ourselves, away from our own environment, and take a bird's-eye view, as it were, of our little world from among the stars; to try to see ourselves as others see us and especially endeavor to view things as they appear from the judgment seat of God. We can hold a candle light so close to our eye as to make it appear larger than the sun: much like a prejudiced judgment. The only thing to do is to hold the candle far enough away so as to view both candle and sun in their proper proportions. In curing ourselves of prejudiced judgments, it is often necessary to change our view entirely. We may have to give up our old way of looking at things. However, even then, we should make good judgment the basis of the compromise.

Sister Mary Cecilia

PART FOUR

Time To Rejoice

*Women of vision rejoice. They praise God, trying—
and not always succeeding—to praise him in all
circumstances. They see the sunshine, take vacations,
relax, have fun, make mistakes, and celebrate
Christmas. Don't you? So here are joyous things,
happy stories to share. Good news.*

Gratitude, thanksgiving, and praise

Celebrating Christmas

There is no time in the Christian year when the home is more important than at Christmas. Christmas is the time to adorn your house, fill it with the food of celebration, and invite those who are alone to come in and share it with you.

No religious feast requires more physical work. Advent is supposed to be a time of meditation and penance, but usually the mother's mortifications are more worldly and more directly linked to the coming celebrations. Celebrating Christmas can involve an enormous amount of work.

This work is an Advent penance of a real, physical, human kind; it is the way mothers put themselves out to show the importance of Jesus' coming in their lives; the way also in which they spread the good news to all—to those to whom they have sent cards, to those to whom they have sung carols, to those to whom they have made a donation, to those who pass their house and see their Christmas tree lit up in the window, to those who share in the turkey they cooked and the cake they made, and most of all to their children, for whom more than anyone the work has been done, because the whole of the festivities is a huge educational aid for the simple but life-changing message, "Jesus Christ is born."

At Christmas, mothers take the lead in preaching the gospel.

Margaret Hebblethwaite

Bathed in light

Childbirth is a peak experience, but not a lying one, not a brief moment of success in a miserable, hopeless world that will soon swallow it up. It is a privileged moment, God-given for our learning so that, remembering what we then saw so clearly, our whole lives after may be bathed in light.

Margaret Hebblethwaite

The sheer loveliness of the world

It seems to me that the very great thing is to be able to enjoy life. When I was in the hospital last year and they told me that they were not at all sure they could operate, I felt no fear of death, though I did not want to die. But what I did feel was remorse, because I realized that I had never really let myself enjoy life—so many scruples and inhibitions and things preventing me from really enjoying the sheer loveliness of the world, the people in it, and even the material things in it, food, drink, the sun, spending money, etc. I made only one resolution: if I was given another chance (as I have been), I would enjoy everything in life that I can, for as long as I can, and as wholly as I can.

Caryll Houselander

Holiday

One of the best things you can do on holiday is to ask nothing, want nothing, but just praise God for everything. Always be praising him—for the little sticky leaves, the rich somber greenness of the trees, all the kindness you get on a holiday. Just one long praise of little beautiful things, and forget that great, big, striving, blundering self of yours. Then come back to us clean and fresh and contagious, and let us too get a sight of the glory of God.

Florence Allshorn

Give thanks

On the very night before they crucified him, Jesus "took the cup and gave thanks." Things were not going well for him that night! But he gave thanks anyway.

Gratitude was the normal state of his heart.

If your life is good, if things are going well for you, if your cup is running over, don't stop with a fleeting period of guilt for not having been thankful enough. No point in wasting time with that. Simply begin to give thanks. Give thanks if your cup is filled with sweetness and drink it with grace. Give thanks also if your cup is only half full or even filled with trouble, and drink it with grace. Grace is available for us under all conditions. Grace to give thanks to our Father. The grace Jesus Christ brings into the human life is never limited by the circumstances of that life.

Eugenia Price

Begin

Ingratitude snaps shut the human heart. Grateful hearts are always open hearts. They are hearts which have received. Even God cannot squeeze a blessing through a closed heart.

We need to form the habit of gratitude. It can change everything! One little start toward being grateful to God for health, for food, for his love, begins at once to make us feel less inferior. If he cares enough to give us these things—maybe we have been exaggerating our pitiable plight! An ungrateful heart is a blind heart. It cannot see its blessings until it begins to give thanks.

Eugenia Price

Say thank you

Gratitude has immense transformational powers—for ourselves, our lives, and our circumstances. I have used this tool over and over again. It has taken me through many stressful circumstances—poverty, divorce, being alone, learning how to date, moves, overwhelming projects, overwhelming feelings, troubles with children, troubles with neighbors, fear, circumstances that perplexed me, and other unlit, foggy parts of this journey. Gratitude helps make things work out well. It helps us feel better while stressful things are happening. Then when things get better, it helps us enjoy the good.

Force gratitude. Say thank you again and again for each circumstance. Say thank you even if you're not feeling grateful. Eventually the power of gratitude will take over, and joy and true gratitude will begin.

Melody Beattie

Expect the good

To those who may feel that I ascribe to faith such simple events, such small happenings, I would say that life is mainly made up of little things, but the fact that they are little does not make them unimportant. Faith can remove molehills as well as mountains, and only by practicing faith continually in the seemingly insignificant things does one develop the power to overcome the big crises when they come. I have learnt that the true practice of faith is really a state of being, a state in which one is unwaveringly expectant of good, and in which one thanks God for benefits before they are actually manifest.

Katie Whitelegg

Cheering us on

We are compassed about by a cloud of witnesses, whose hearts throb in sympathy with every effort and struggle, and who thrill with joy at every success. How should this thought check and rebuke every worldly feeling and unworthy purpose, and enshrine us, in the midst of a forgetful and unspiritual world, with an atmosphere of heavenly peace! They have overcome—have risen—are crowned, glorified; but still they remain to us, our assistants, our comforters, and in every hour of darkness their voice speaks to us: "So we grieved, so we struggled, so we fainted, so we doubted; but we have overcome, we have obtained, we have seen, we have found—and in our victory behold the certainty of thy own."

Harriet Beecher Stowe

The God of all happiness

[God says:] "Consider attentively that as I am your God, so am I infinitely good. I cannot will anything but that which is useful and salutary to you and to all; nor can I wish any evil to my creatures. Thus illuminated by the living light of faith, you will perceive that I, your God, have infinitely more knowledge, power, and will to advance your happiness than you have. Therefore seek with all diligence to submit yourself totally to my will; so shall you abide in continual tranquillity of spirit, and shall have me forever with you."

Saint Catherine of Siena

The goodness of God

Jesus, my center and life

In returning thanks I will approach my Savior as a wounded hart who has come to the fountain, and I will say to him: "God of my soul, O Jesus, Fountain of milk and honey, Spouse of pure souls, Love without limit, I have dared to approach you—I, who am nothing, you, who are riches infinite; I, who am sick, you, who are the best of physicians; I, who am full of uncleanness, you, who are the mirror of purity; I, who am a vessel of miseries, you, who are the Father of Mercies. Urged by my great need, I draw nigh to you, the Source of safety, sweetness, comfort. Behold, I hide myself wholly in your generous heart, while confessing that I am not worthy even to present myself before your eyes, O Heavenly Beauty, Infinite Purity, Inexhaustible Well of Sanctity, from which all other sanctity flows. O Burning Sun of Divine Charity, illumine my soul by your presence! O Infinite Beauty and Loneliness, when shall you sanctify my soul, when transform me into yourself, when, alas, O Sweetness of my heart, my most loving Jesus and God? O strange and wonderful—so ungrateful and blind is this heart of mine that it never rightly values the precious and sublime gift which the Almighty communicated to me this day! My Jesus, I thank you for having satiated me with your own self, O Immeasurable Good. I bless you, I give you thanks, my Jesus; I praise you, O Boundless Love, Heavenly Drink, Delicious Food, Never-failing Wealth, Incomparable Nobility, Perpetual Joy, Center and Life of my Soul!"

Blessed Mary of the Angels

Drinking draughts of God

We have grown up with a Christianity that has little room for the physical, both in terms of human bodies and in terms of places to put them. Our thinkers and guides have for centuries been men without a wife and family, and without a home unless it be a monastery. Yes, if it comes to a monastery we have learned to find the sacred in it. Monasteries are places that speak to us of God just by our walking around them. But we have not learned to relate to the sacred in the family home, so that just by walking around the house of a Christian family we can feel we are drinking in draughts of God. We have not dared to think in those terms.

Margaret Hebblethwaite

God loves us as we are

When Jesus told the man on the pallet that his sins were forgiven, he was in effect saying this: "It is all right to be you. I love you as you are and God loves you as you are. We understand your weakness and vulnerability. There is no need to be afraid and bury yourself under masks, because God and I love all those aspects of yourself that you have made into your shadow side, we love the maskless you utterly and unconditionally. So there is no need to be weighted down by guilt, alienation, and despair. Be yourself: live your life honestly, openly, and fearlessly because we will never reject you. But if you slip back into the shadows, do not worry, because we are with you in the darkness and want to bring you back into the light." Forgiveness is the love and acceptance of people as they are.

Elizabeth Stuart

God is there

Any relationship based upon love and acceptance can become sacramental. *Ubi caritas et amore, Deus ibi est*—where charity and love are found, God is there.

Elizabeth Stuart

Ah, Mary we hardly know you

Ah, Mary we hardly know you—
A few tantalizing glimpses
relegated by most to "introduction"
useful to lead into the "real" story,
relegated to the task and place of women—
standing by and watching over,
caring for needs,
keeping a death watch,
providing loving care
for the body of the dead one,
the child of your womb.
Ah, Mary we discover you—
one who was open and receptive—
open to the love and mercy of God,
open to embodiment of the living word,
receptive to life,
you became filled with life.
Ah, Mary you have become the glory of God—
"The glory of God is a human being fully alive."
You are the glory of God!
Ah, Mary we hardly knew you—
A few tantalizing glimpses,
but we look at you afresh
and in you begin to see ourselves.

We are the dwelling place of God.
We are the glory of God.
Thanks be to God!

Karen Summers

My angel

I have only ever seen an angel once. It was on a rainy day when I was eight years old. I had been kept indoors all morning, but at last the clouds cleared a little, the rain stopped, and I went out to play. No one was about, so I filled the time waiting for my friends by throwing a ball up against the side of the house. Then I looked up and saw the angel—high above me, robed in white, haloed in gold and floating across a sky that had suddenly cleared to a violet blue.

I ran to call my mother to come and see my angel. She was busy and had no time to come just at that moment, but she said, "You are very lucky to see that angel. Not many people see them. I expect if I came I would see only a cloud, edged with sunshine in a rainy sky. But you have seen an angel."

"What is an angel?" I asked her.

"It really means a messenger of God," she said, "and God sends messages to us in many ways. Your angel is telling you what a beautiful place the world can be, even on a rainy day."

Pauline Webb

Believe in God and make someone happy

If I have any message to leave, it is this: Believe in God. He guides and protects you all through life, as I trust this account of my life has demonstrated. Discipline yourself daily by having a plan—not just vague, wishful thinking. Commit yourself daily to doing something, however small, for somebody else, for by making other people happy you will find true happiness yourself.

Olave, Lady Baden-Powell

God understands

God is not malicious. Not punitive. Not a trickster. Not out to play jokes on us. God may ask us to wait longer than we want, but only if waiting is in our best interest.

God knows our hearts and God understands our healing needs. God understands the good that is waiting around the corner for us, the good that we can't see yet. God sees the benefit in the lessons we're learning, not just the turmoil, which is what we so often focus on.

God can help us bring out the healer in ourselves.

Melody Beattie

God loves and keeps us

He showed a little thing, the quantity of a hazelnut, lying in the palm of my hand, as meseemed, and it was as round as a ball. I looked thereon with the eye of my understanding, and thought, "What may this be?" and it was answered generally thus, "It is all that is made." I marveled how it might last; for methought it might suddenly have fallen to naught for littleness. And I was answered in my understanding, "It lasts, and ever shall: for God loved it. And so hath all things being by the Love of God." In this little thing I saw three properties. The first is, that God made it. The second is, that God loves it. The third is, that God keeps it. For this is the cause which we be not all in ease of heart and soul: for we seek here rest in this thing which is so little, where no rest is in; and we know not our God that is all Might, all Wise, and all Good, for his is very rest. God wills to be known, and it pleases him that we rest in him. For all that is beneath him satisfies us not.

Blessed Julian of Norwich

God's goodness to women

Jesus said to the two Marys: "All hail!" And they came and held him by the feet, and worshiped him. Then said Jesus unto them, "Be not afraid: go, tell my brethren that they go into Galilee, and there shall they see me" (Matthew 28:9, 10). There are two or three points in this beautiful narrative to which we wish to call the attention of our readers.

First, it was the first announcement of the glorious news to a lost world and a company of forsaking disciples. Second, it was as public as the nature of the case demanded; and intended ultimately to be published to the ends of the earth. Third, Mary was expressly commissioned to reveal the fact to the apostles; and thus she literally became their teacher on that memorable occasion. Oh, glorious privilege, to be allowed to herald the glad tidings of a Savior risen! How could it be that our Lord chose a woman to this honor? Well, one reason might be that the male disciples were all missing at the time. They all forsook him, and fled. But woman was there, as she had ever been, ready to minister to her risen, as to her dying, Lord.

But, surely, if the dignity of our Lord or his message were likely to be imperiled by committing this sacred trust to a woman, he who was guarded by legions of angels could have commanded another messenger; but, as if intent on doing her honor, and rewarding her unwavering fidelity, he reveals himself first to her; and, as an evidence that he had taken out of the way the curse under which she had so long groaned, nailing it to his cross, he makes her who had been first in the transgression first also in the glorious knowledge of complete redemption.

Catherine Booth

Certain of God's help

When I was about seven years old, I announced that my favorite text was "Hitherto hath the Lord helped me." The elders were amused, but I am not so sure that it was funny after all. Looking back over many years, I fancy my choice now would be much the same. I am not prepared, here and now, to analyze and define the reasons, but I can only say that this quiet certainty has run all through my life, linking up babyhood and youth and middle age with the latest stretch of the road. And "hitherto," though sometimes almost slipping through one's fingers, that golden thread has never wholly escaped my grasp.

Elizabeth Fox Howard

God's love is everywhere

There is no need for anyone to press upon me the reality of hell as the early Calvinists did with stony hearts, for I have been in hell; but having been there myself, I am driven to believe that there is love below all.

Josephine Butler

The soul experiences life

The soul's state of union with the sacred Person of the
Word unites it with the very source of light in regard to
every truth and causes it to live under its influence. It is of
this pasture that the divine Savior spoke when he said: I am
the good Shepherd. If anyone enter by me who am the
gate, he shall come in and go out and shall find pasture.
And thus the soul has life in him and from him in a
delightful way, which is better experienced than described.

Blessed Marie of the Incarnation

Look forward

The coming of the Kingdom is perpetual—the real Christian is always a revolutionary—God is with the future.

Evelyn Underhill

The goodness of created things

It is doubtless a good thing to set aside material imaginings, since spiritual persons say that it is so, but in my opinion, this should not be attempted before the soul is very far advanced, as it is clear that till then, it ought to seek the Creator by means of creatures. To do otherwise is to act as if we were angels.

Saint Teresa of Ávila

Seeing God face-to-face

God within us

You already know that God is in all places; now it is clear, that where the king is, there is the court; in a word, that where God is, there heaven is: you may also believe without doubting, that where his Majesty is, all his glory is.

Consider what St. Augustine says, that he sought God in many places, and came at last to find him in himself. Do you think it is of little importance for a distracted soul to understand this truth, and to know that she need not go to heaven to speak with her eternal Father, or to regale herself with him? Nor need she speak aloud, for however low she may speak, he is so near that he will hear us; neither does she require wings to fly and seek him, but she can compose herself in solitude and behold him within herself. And let her not separate from so good a Guest, but with great humility speak to him as a Father, entreat him as a Father, relate her troubles to him, and beg a remedy for them, knowing that she is not worthy to be his daughter.

Saint Teresa of Ávila

Accept God's graces

Be on your guard, daughter, against a certain false modesty, to which some persons are addicted, and think it is humility. Yet it is *not* humility, if the King is pleased to show you a favor, not to accept of it. But it is humility to accept it, and acknowledge how much it exceeds your merits, and so you may rejoice in it. A fine humility indeed!—that I should entertain in my house the Emperor of heaven and earth, who comes therein to show me kindness and recreate himself with me, while I out of humility will neither answer him, nor stay with him, nor accept what he gives me, but leave him there alone. And though he may bid and entreat me to ask him for something, I through humility must remain poor, and even allow him to go away, because he sees I have not determined on anything!

Pay no attention to such humility, daughters, but treat with him as with a father, as with a brother, as with a lord, as with a spouse, sometimes in one way, sometimes in another, for he will teach you what you should do to please him. Be not too easy, but challenge his word, since he is your spouse, that he would treat you as such.

Saint Teresa of Ávila

The interior castle

Within us there is a palace of immense magnificence: the whole building is of gold and precious stones; in a word, it is every way as it ought to be for such a Lord. Forget not, also, that you are partly the cause that this edifice is such as it is; for truly there is no building of such great beauty as a pure soul, filled with virtues; and the greater these virtues are, the brighter do these stones sparkle; and that in this palace the great King lodges, who has been pleased to become your Guest; and that he sits there on the throne of immense value, which is your heart. This may, at first, seem ridiculous (I mean to make use of such a figure to make you understand what I say). Still it may be of great help to you especially; for since we women want learning, all this is indeed very necessary to make us understand that there is within us something else more precious beyond comparison than that which we see outwardly. Let us not imagine we have nothing in our interior.

Saint Teresa of Ávila

What the heart enjoys with her God

When I went to holy Communion, it seemed that the door of my heart was thrown wide open, as if for the purpose of receiving a friend; and as soon as he had entered, it was closed. Thus it came to pass that my heart shut itself up alone with its God. It is out of my power to describe all the effects and movements and exultations that his presence produced. If I were to give to you as an illustration every pastime and pleasure that our dearest friends could provide for us, I should say they are nothing in comparison; and if all the joys the universe can afford were united, I should pronounce them nothing when compared with what my heart enjoys with her God, or rather with what God works in my soul, for it is all his own operation. Love causes the heart to dance and leap for joy, to sing and to be silent according as it pleases; love soothes it to repose, or wakes it to triumphant bliss; love sets it vigorously to work afresh for its God; love possesses it, and it yields to all; love rules it, and it rests.

Saint Veronica Giuliani

The palace of love

The holy Eucharist is the very palace and sanctuary of love.
The heart becomes inflamed when it sees itself the
dwelling place of the most holy Trinity; and when Jesus
comes to me in the Blessed Sacrament, and I hear the
words, "Hail thou temple of the whole Trinity!" then my
heart becomes so enlarged and enkindled that sometimes I
seem to hear sweet melodies, and am ravished with heavenly
music. When engaged in laborious duties, I find myself
ready to do anything.

Saint Veronica Giuliani

All shall be well

In our very Mother, Jesus, our life is grounded, in the fore-seeing Wisdom of himself from without beginning, with the high Might of the Father, the high sovereign Goodness of the Holy Ghost.

Fair and sweet is our heavenly Mother in the sight of our souls; precious and lovely are the Gracious Children in the sight of our heavenly Mother, with mildness and meekness, and all the fair virtues that belong to children in Nature. For of nature the Child despairs not of the Mother's love, of nature the Child presumes not of itself, of nature the Child loves the Mother and each one of the other children. These are the fair virtues, with all other that be like, wherewith our heavenly Mother is served and pleased.

And I understood none higher statue in this life than Childhood, in feebleness and failing of might and of wit, unto the time that our Gracious Mother has brought us up to our Father's bliss. And then shall it verily be known to us his meaning in those sweet words where he says: All shall be well; and thou shall see, thyself, that all manner of things shall be well.

I understood that all his blessed children which be come out of him by Nature shall be brought again into him by Grace.

Blessed Julian of Norwich

Prayer and a learned lady

[The Lord said,] "Let her endeavor, at least for one hour each day, in the morning or evening, or whenever she finds it most suitable, to separate herself from all exterior things, and to recollect herself interiorly, to think of me and know my will; and let her thus exercise herself devoutly, as far as she can during the time she has chosen, in all that I inspire her with; whether it be praise, thanksgiving for the special favors I have bestowed on her, or for those which I have granted to others, or prayer for sinners, or for the souls in purgatory."

Saint Gertrude the Great

God is my being

Whenever God can do so, he attracts the human free will
by sweet allurements, and afterward disposes it in such a
manner that all things may conduce to the annihilation of
man's proper being. So that in God is my being, my *me*, my
strength, my beatitude, my good, and my delight. I say *mine*
at present because it is not possible to speak otherwise; but
I do not mean by it any such thing as *me* or *mine*, or delight
or good, or strength or stability, or beatitude: nor could I
possibly turn my eyes to behold such things in heaven or in
earth. And if, notwithstanding, I sometimes use words that
may have the likeness of humility and of spirituality, in my
interior I do not understand them, I do not feel them. In
truth it astonishes me that I speak at all, or use words so far
removed from the truth and from that which I feel. I see
clearly that man in this world deceives himself by admiring
and esteeming things which are not, and neither sees nor
esteems things which are.

Saint Catherine of Genoa

Union with God

Whatever be the degree of union with God which the soul experiences in this life, there always remains a higher degree of union, God being infinite in his gifts. Here is an example: Before I became a religious, even before his divine Majesty had given me the knowledge and graces relative to the most Holy Trinity that I've mentioned, the lights which I had from Holy Scripture begot in me a faith so vivid that it seemed to me that I would have passed through flames on behalf of these truths, such was the degree to which I grasped their certainty and their efficacy. They afforded me a hope that I would not only possess and enjoy the good things which had been manifested to me in God but distinct from him, and God himself, but that I would do so for the sake of this same God and his glory. This hope caused me to forget myself in order to please my divine Spouse; it led me to do things and to subject myself to dangers which surpassed everything that a person of my sex could do.

The graces and favors which his divine Majesty has granted me were graces always conducive to higher perfection and to spiritual advancement.

Blessed Marie of the Incarnation

Come into my soul

Come, O King of Heaven, prepare my heart by purifying my conscience, that I may worthily go to meet you. Come, O God of Armies, to bless me and give me your peace, and all my soul will be in peace. Come, Eternal Wisdom, instruct me in holy fear, and teach me the way to heaven. O Good Shepherd, come and seek for the wandering sheep and save it. You are our Lawgiver: come and impress on my heart the love of your holy precepts; you are the King of nations: come and reign over all my affections; you are the King of Israel: come and take complete possession of my heart; you are the Key of David: come and open to me the treasures of your mercy; you are the splendor of the glory of the Father: come and display to my eyes the radiance of your virtues. In a word, descend, O divine Word, from the bosom of the Eternal Father to the womb of Mary, and from the bosom of Mary come—ah come!—into my soul.

Blessed Mary of the Angels

Timeless existence

I saw this truth very clearly: Eternity is not an infinite succession of moments including past and future. It has neither past, nor present, nor future. It is existence, pure and simple, without any idea of time.

Lucie Christine

About the Contributors

Eighty-five women are represented in this volume—contemporary women and women who lived hundreds of years ago; Catholic, Protestant, and Orthodox women; homemakers and doctors of the Church. Here is more information about some of them.

Saint Agnes. Agnes was martyred in fourth-century Rome as a young teen, after refusing a marriage proposal.

Sylvia Mary Alison. Founder of the Prison Fellowship in England, Alison was also involved in the foundation of the Prison Fellowship in Northern Ireland, Scotland, Canada, New Zealand, and Australia. She is the wife of Conservative MP Michael Alison.

Florence Allshorn (1887–1950). She served as a missionary in Uganda. After she returned to England, she spent twelve years training missionaries. She founded the St. Julian's Community as a place of restoration and further study for missionaries on home leave.

Olave, Lady Baden-Powell (1889–1977). Born in England, at the age of twenty-three she became engaged to the fifty-five-year-old founder of the Boy Scouts and Girl Guides. She traveled with her husband and, after his death, alone, to continue his work.

Margaret Fairless Barber (1869–1901). Under the pseudonym Michael Fairless, she wrote serialized short novels, including *The Roadmender* and *The Gathering of Brother Hilarius.*

Melody Beattie. As an author, she has liberated countless troubled and damaged people through her books on codependency and bereavement.

Lin Berwick. Berwick is an author, counselor, and Methodist lay preacher, even as she struggles with physical disabilities, including cerebral palsy and blindness.

Saint Julie Billiart (1751–1816). A down-to-earth peasant woman of enormous faith, humor, and stamina, she opened schools in France and Belgium, founding the Sisters of Notre Dame de Namur to teach and care for the pupils.

Elizabeth Blackwell (1821–1910). The first woman to qualify as a medical doctor in the United States (1849). Deeply religious, she devoted her life to work among the poorest of women and children. After much opposition, she founded a hospital for training women medical students, which opened on Florence Nightingale's birthday.

Margaret Blagge (1652–1677). Because her father had a position at court, Blagge was, at age sixteen, a lady-in-waiting at the court of Charles II. Devout and pious, she was also a talented actress and a general favorite, whose diary reveals how she strove to live a Christian life in a very worldly, dissolute environment. She married the Earl of Godolphin and was blissfully happy in her marriage. She died in childbirth at the age of twenty-five.

Margaret Bondfield (1873–1953). Born in Somerset, England, Bondfield's trade-union work led her into Labor politics. She was chairman of the Trades Union Congress in 1923 and the first woman cabinet minister as Minister of Labor from 1929–1931.

Corrie ten Boom (1892–1983). Ten Boom was a young woman and the daughter of a Dutch watchmaker when Germany invaded Holland. She became involved in the work to enable persecuted Jews to escape, and as a result she was imprisoned in the concentration camp at Ravensbrück, where her sister died. Out of her sufferings came a ministry of hope and reconciliation.

Catherine Booth (1829–1890). She is known as the "mother" of the Salvation Army. With her husband, William, she started the Church Mission in London in 1865, which became known as the Salvation Army in 1878. She realized that the outcasts they sought to help would never be found in churches or chapels but had to be met in their own hovels. Her talent as a preacher—and the novelty at that time of hearing a woman preach—provided much interest and funding for the work, and she was strongly supported in this by her husband.

Maria Boulding. A contemplative nun at Stanbrook Abbey, Boulding is the author of several books.

Saint Bridget of Sweden (1302–1373). She was a lady-in-waiting in the queen's court and mother of eight children. When widowed, she founded the Brigittine order, served the poor, and was outspoken in her advice to the pope and to royalty.

Josephine Butler (1828–1906). Born into a privileged and shel-tered English family, this witty and intelligent woman always had a deep concern for the sufferings of others. She married George Butler, who became assistant principal of Cheltenham College and then principal of Liverpool College. It was in Liverpool that Josephine came into contact with prostitutes, and their welfare became her major concern, which shocked polite society. A prominent Anglican lay woman, Butler was a lifelong campaigner for women's rights and suffrage.

Joan Porter Buxton. After the early death of her father in Egypt, Joan was adopted into an upper-class family in the early 1900s. Her book, *You've Got to Take a Chance!*, tells the story of her difficult early years and of how she came to terms with the loss of identity and the confusion resulting from being told rather cruelly at the age of twelve that she was adopted. Her story continues with the rediscovery of her mother, her coming to faith, and her final years of reconciliation and happiness.

Amy Carmichael (1868–1951). Born in Northern Ireland, she felt called by God to go to India. She founded the Dohnavur Fellowship in South India, which rescued children sold into Hindu temple service. She wrote many books and poems despite much ill health during her later years.

Saint Catherine of Genoa (1447–1510). She was a wealthy married woman and a mystic. After her spiritual conversion in 1473, Catherine devoted her life to hospital work and church reform.

Saint Catherine of Siena (1347–1380). A third-order Dominican and mystic, she was named a Doctor of the Church for her profound writings. She tried to broker peace in Europe and worked with the sick and poor.

Lucie Christine (1844–1908). Lucie Christine is the pseudonym of a wealthy French woman, mother of five, who kept copious spiritual journals of her mystical relationship with Christ.

Saint Clare of Assisi (ca. 1193–1253). A native of Assisi, she was inspired by God and the example of Saint Francis to found monasteries of sisters in Italy, France, and Germany.

Kate Compston. A minister of the United Reformed Church (based in Hampshire, England), Compston is a writer of prayers, poems, and meditations.

Elizabeth L. Comstock (1815–1890). An English member of the Society of Friends, she traveled to America, where Abraham Lincoln arranged for her to have free access to all hospitals. There she worked with the wounded of both armies during the Civil War and with soldiers in army prisons.

Margaret Cundiff. A popular writer and broadcaster, Cundiff has served on the staff of St. James' Church, Selby, North Yorkshire, England, since 1973. In 1987 she was ordained a deacon and later priest.

Mary Endersbee. Born in Cheshire, England, she became assistant editor of *Crusade* magazine after recovering from a nervous breakdown.

Betty Ford. Known most publicly as the wife of Gerald Ford, former president of the United States, her place in this book comes from her own courage and religious faith, drawn on during her battle with drug addiction and alcoholism. The Betty Ford Center in Rancho Mirage, California, has brought hope and recovery to many.

Elizabeth Fry (1780–1845). An English Quaker who, even after raising eleven children and founding a school for children, felt that she was still doing too little with her life. In 1813, a visiting American Quaker took her to see Newgate Prison. Fry was so horrified by the appalling conditions of the women prisoners that she dedicated herself to helping them. She provided decent clothing, taught the prisoners to teach their children, and organized support groups of prisoners to help them prepare for and endure being transported overseas for their crimes. To give them comfort and moral support, she accompanied the women to every convict ship that left London for nearly twenty years until her death.

Saint Gertrude the Great (ca. 1256–ca. 1302). She lived from childhood at a Benedictine convent in Helfta, Germany. Like many mystics, she felt chosen as the bride of Christ, and her counsel was widely respected.

Saint Veronica Giuliani (1660–1727). A level-headed Capuchin abbess-administrator, she was also known for experiencing some of the most extreme mystical phenomena.

Madame Guyon (1648–1717). A widow and mystic whose spiritual writings and teaching prompted a five-year stint in the Bastille prison, which broke her health.

Valerie Hadert. Hadert takes a lively interest in her local church and writes verse, some of which has been published in *Challenge* and *Decision*. Her work has also served as the inspiration for a number of songs by British pop star Cliff Richard. Afflicted with multiple sclerosis, Hadert now resides in a hospital near London.

Frances Ridley Havergal (1836–1879). An Anglican poet and hymn writer who was prolific in five languages and eventually memorized nearly all of the New Testament.

Margaret Hebblethwaite. London born, she read theology and philosophy at Oxford University and studied spirituality at the Gregorian University, Rome. Her book *Motherhood and God* marries her theological training with her own experience as a mother of two small, lively children.

Margaret Holden. She was arrested for sharing in a vigil of silent prayer on the steps of the Ministry of Defense, Whitehall, London.

Caryll Houselander (1901–1954). She was a prolific Roman Catholic writer of prose and poetry. Her biographer, Maisie Sheed, wrote: "Her books sold like novels . . . not offering help to her readers as the fruit of her own victory but inviting them to join her in a battle that she was fighting to the very end of her life. . . . It was from conscious weakness not from strength that she brought to others the power of God's love."

Elizabeth Fox Howard (1873–1957). A Quaker since age thirty, Howard was active in various humanitarian causes. During World War I, she was the visiting Quaker chaplain to conscientious objectors in prison and also worked on behalf of "enemy aliens."

Blessed Julian of Norwich (ca. 1342–ca. 1420). A contemporary of Chaucer, she was perhaps the only Englishwoman generally accepted as a great mystic of the medieval church. During a near-fatal illness in 1373, she received sixteen visions, which she carefully recorded. Over the following years, she meditated on them and eventually produced a revised and expanded version entitled *Revelations of Divine Love.* She lived as an anchoress in a small cell attached to the wall of the Church of St. Edmund and St. Julian in Norwich, East Anglia, where she received and advised visitors who came to her window.

Catherine Marshall LeSourd (1914–1983). A well-known American writer whose book *Christy* has inspired movies and a television series. After her first husband, Peter Marshall, died, leaving her a young widow with two young children, she wrote his life story in *A Man Called Peter.* Later books chronicled her life of faith, her work, and her subsequent remarriage and family life.

Victoria Lidiard. An English woman who was active in the Women's Social and Political Union, a suffragette organization. Trained as an optician, she was the first woman on the honorary staff of the London Refraction Hospital. She was also a first committee member of the Anglican Welfare of Animals Society and active in many animal welfare organizations.

Blessed Marie of the Incarnation (1599–1672). A French widow and businesswoman, Marie Martin left her adolescent son with her sister and joined an Ursuline convent. An intense mystic, she felt called to join the first female missionaries to Quebec, where she became prioress.

Sister Mary Cecilia. A member of Ursuline Convent of Our Lady of Lourdes in Paola, Kansas, Sister Mary is the author of *Efficiency in the Spiritual Life*, published in 1921.

Blessed Mary of the Angels (1661–1717). Born into Italian nobility, she entered a Discalced Carmelite convent, where she was known as a mystic, prioress, prophet, and advisor to royalty.

Saint Mechthild of Magdeburg (ca. 1212–ca. 1282). A German mystic who lived a hermit-like existence, she wrote down her visions and revelations for almost twenty years before becoming a Cistercian nun.

Dame Gertrude More (d. 1633). A Benedictine nun at Cambray, France, Dame Gertrude was a relative of the British martyr Sir Thomas More.

Hannah More (1745–1833). She was an Anglican religious writer and philanthropist and a friend of William Wilberforce and John Newton. Her plays found great success on the London stage, but she committed herself to providing schools for mining villages and friendly societies to relieve the poverty and hardship she discovered there. Her writings were aimed at the wealthy classes to stir their conscience; she reached the poorer, ordinary folk via the lively Cheap Repository Tracts that she wrote and published.

Janet Morley. An adult education adviser at Christian Aid, this writer and editor has significantly contributed to the cause of women's ministry in the Church of England.

Florence Nightingale (1820–1910). A famous English hospital reformer, she first worked as a nurse in 1851 and served exhaustively abroad during the Crimean War. Florence was a superb administrator, and her practical talents were balanced and nourished by her deep religious faith. The strong mystical leanings she felt always had to be translated into appropriate action.

Anne Ortlund. She is an American writer of Christian books on faith, the family, and the life of the Christian woman. Married to a pastor, she has three adult children.

Saint Perpetua (d. 203). A young North African mother separated from her nursing infant and martyred in a Carthage coliseum. She wrote an account of visions that comforted her when she was facing death.

Barbara Piller. Formerly Mrs. Barbara Clayton, she was a nurse with CMS in Rwanda. A few weeks after she gave birth to their first child, her husband, John Clayton, was shot by Rwandan refugees who had been persuaded to rob them.

Eugenia Price (1916–1996). She was a successful American television producer when she became a Christian at the age of thirty-three. From that moment, she began an outstanding ministry of writing and broadcasting.

Joan Puls, O.S.F. An American Franciscan, she lives in an ecumenical community in Norfolk and conducts retreats. She has written and cowritten a number of books.

Sue Ryder. Lady Ryder of Warsaw CMG, OBE is an English philanthropist and promoter of residential care for the sick and disabled. Her experiences with the First Nursing Yeomanry during the Second World War and later with the Polish section of the Special Operations Executive provided the vision of creating a "living memorial" to those who died and to those, such as refugees, who continued to suffer as a result of the war. She established the Sue Ryder Foundation in 1953.

May Sarton (1912–1995). An internationally acclaimed poet and novelist, this American authored several much-loved and popular journals, including those chronicling her life and struggles in old age and following a stroke.

Cicely Saunders. Dame Saunders is the English pioneer of the modern hospice movement, contributing research and teaching a new approach to caring, particularly for families. She trained at St. Thomas' Hospital Medical School and the Nightingale School of Nursing. She founded St. Christopher's Hospice in Sydenham in 1967 to promote the principles of dying with dignity.

Dorothy L. Sayers (1893–1957). An Englishwoman who wrote detective stories featuring aristocratic detective Lord Peter Wimsey. After graduating from Oxford University, she worked for about ten years as a copywriter for an advertising agency, during which time she wrote most of her detective fiction. Her reputation as a Christian apologist and playwright is crowned by the series *The Man Born to be King*, which was broadcast by the BBC in 1941–42 during the children's hour.

Katharina von Schlegel (b. 1697). She is believed to have been a Lutheran nun.

Aida Skripnikova. Arrested for distributing hand-printed Gospel tracts in Leningrad, she spent a number of years in prison for her faith. She suffered the loss of her job as a lab assistant and was forced to work on a building site. After various arrests and trials and a brief forced detention in a psychiatric clinic, in 1968 she was sentenced to three years in prison.

Hannah Whitall Smith (1832–1911). She wrote one of America's classic inspirational books, *The Christian's Secret of a Happy Life*. Born into a Quaker family, she was a founding member of the Woman's Christian Temperance Union and the women's suffrage movement.

JoAnn Kelley Smith (d. 1974). She described herself as "A Dying Person" in the period during which she and her family coped with the cancer that finally took her life.

Dorothee Soelle. She is a theologian and author, born in Cologne and now living in Hamburg.

Harriet Beecher Stowe (1811–1896). She is best known for writing the novel *Uncle Tom's Cabin.*

Elizabeth Stuart. Born to an Anglican father and a Catholic mother, she studied theology at Oxford and now lectures at the College of St. Mark and St. John in Plymouth, England.

Saint Teresa of Ávila (1515–1582). A Spanish nun and church reformer, she wrote extensively about prayer and was the first woman to be named Doctor of the Church.

Mother Teresa of Calcutta (1910–1997). Born Agnes Gonxha Bojaxhiu to Albanian peasant parents living in Yugoslavia, she went to Ireland in 1928 to become a nun and was sent to India the next year. She spent twenty years teaching in Calcutta before the call came to serve the people of the slums. "The biggest disease today is not leprosy or tuberculosis, but rather the feeling of being unwanted, uncared for, deserted by everybody." In 1949 she founded the Missionaries of Charity, a community of sisters, priests, and brothers who serve the poor. In 1979, she received the Nobel Peace Prize for her work.

Saint Thérèse of Lisieux (1873–1897). Taken from the text of her journal, the best-selling book, *Story of a Soul,* recounts her life as a pampered child and as a young cloistered Carmelite suffering from tuberculosis.

Harriet Tubman (ca. 1820–1913). She escaped slavery in Maryland in 1849 and then returned to the South numerous times to help more than three hundred slaves get to freedom on the Underground Railroad.

Evelyn Underhill (1875–1941). An Anglican lay woman who wrote extensively about mysticism and the spiritual life, she acted as a spiritual director and also led retreats. Her work emphasized the importance of training and discipline and that contemplation should always lead to action.

Blessed Baptista Varani (1458–1527). Abbess of a Poor Clare convent built by her father (the duke of Camerino, Italy), she knew the heights and depths of mystical ecstasy.

Pauline Webb. A broadcaster and writer, she was born in London and has traveled extensively. Former vice president of the Methodist Conference, she was vice moderator of the World Council of Churches from 1968 until 1975.

Index of Authors

Index of Subjects

Acknowledgments

We would like to thank all those who have given us permission to include quotations in this book, as indicated in the list below. Every effort has been made to trace and contact copyright owners. If there are any inadvertent omissions or errors in the acknowledgments, we apologize to those concerned and will remedy these in the next edition.

Sylvia Mary Alison: from *God Is Building a House*, Marshall Morgan & Scott, 1984.

Olave, Lady Baden-Powell: from Mary Drewery, *Window on My Heart*, copyright © 1973 by Lady Baden-Powell and Mary Drewery. Reproduced by permission of Hodder & Stoughton Ltd.

Melody Beattie: extract from *Codependents' Guide to the Twelve Steps*, published by Piatkus Books and Simon and Schuster.

Evelyn Bence: from *Priscilla Papers*, fall 1994. Used by permission of Evelyn Bence.

Margaret Bondfield: from *What Life Has Taught Me*, Odhams.

Amy Carmichael: from *Candles in the Dark*, copyright © 1981 The Dohnavur Fellowship, London: 1982 Christian Literature Crusade, Ft. Washington. Used by permission.

Gwen Cashmore: from *Clearing the Way* by Gwen Cashmore and Joan Puls O.S.F., WCC Publications, World Council of Churches, Geneva, Switzerland. Used with permission.

Cassell plc: from Margaret Hebblethwaite, *Motherhood and God*, Geoffrey Chapman, 1984; from Lucy Menzies, *Mirror of the Holy*, Mowbray, 1928, for Mechthild of Magdeburg; from

Dorothee Soelle (tr. Joyce Irwin), *Celebrating Resistance*, Mowbray, 1993.

Christian Aid/SPCK: from *Bread of Tomorrow*, Janet Morley.

Kate Compston: from *Encompassing Presence, the Prayer Handbook*, 1993, and *A Restless Hope, the Prayer Handbook*, 1995, published by the United Reformed Church.

The Congregational Federation: from Marion Beales, "News Share," published in *A Restless Hope, the Prayer Handbook*, 1995.

Mary Craig: *Blessings*. Copyright © 1979 by Mary Craig. Reproduced by permission of Hodder & Stoughton Ltd.

Darton, Longman and Todd: from *Beyond the Horizon*, Cicely Saunders.

An elderly widow: from *The View in Winter*, Allen Lane, 1979. Copyright © Ronald Blythe, 1979. Reproduced by permission of the author c/o Rogers, Coleridge & White Ltd., 20 Powis Mews, London WI I IJN.

Mary Endersbee: from *Taught by Pain*, Falcon Books, 1972.

Betty Ford: from *Betty: A Glad Awakening* by Betty Ford with Chris Chase, Jove/Doubleday, 1988.

The Grail Publications: from The Grail Society.

Emilie Griffin: from The Chrysostom Society, *Stories for the Christian Year.* New York: Collier/Macmillan 1992. Used by permission of Emilie Griffin.

Grosvenor Books: from Joan Porter Buxton, *You've Got to Take a Chance!*

Valerie Hadert: from *Taught by Pain,* ed. Mary Endersbee, Falcon Books, 1972.

HarperCollins Publishers: from *Gateway to Hope,* Maria Boulding; from *Child of My Love,* Sue Ryder; from *Celebration,* Margaret Spufford; from *Through Brokenness,* Elizabeth Stuart; from *Candles for Advent,* Pauline Webb.

Enid Henke: from *Beyond the Horizon,* ed. Cicely Saunders, Darton, Longman and Todd, 1989.

Josephine Hilton: from *Claiming God's Promises,* ed. Catherine Marshall, Hodder & Stoughton, 1973.

R. A. Hodgkin: from Mary F. Smith, *A Sacramental Approach to Modern Life,* published by the Society of Friends.

Margaret Holden: from *All the Glorious Names, the Prayer Handbook,* 1989, published by the United Reformed Church.

Michael Howard: from Elizabeth Fox Howard.

Arthur James: from Lin Berwick, *Inner Vision,* Arthur James Ltd, 1990.

Keston Institute: from *Aida of Leningrad,* eds. Xenia Howard-Johnston and Michael Bourdeaux, Gateway Outreach: Aida Skripnikova.

Kingsway Communications: from Corrie ten Boom, *Amazing Love.*

Victoria Lidiard: from *Christianity: Faith, Love and Healing,* Vantage Press, 1985.

Catherine Marshall: p. 90 from *Meeting God at Every Turn.* Reproduced by permission of Hodder & Stoughton Ltd (copyright © 1981), and Chosen Books, USA; pp. 41, 99 from *Claiming God's Promises* by Catherine Marshall and others, Hodder & Stoughton, 1981.

Kate McIlhagga: from *Encompassing Presence, the Prayer Handbook,* 1995, published by the United Reformed Church.

Nelson Word UK: from *Disciplines of the Beautiful Woman,* Anne Ortlund.

Barbara Piller: from *Taught by Pain,* ed. Mary Endersbee, Falcon Books, 1972.

Eugenia Price: pp. 47, 93, 125, 185, 206, 207 from *A Woman's Choice,* Oliphants, 1962; pp. 33, 37 from *The Burden Is Light,* Jove/Doubleday, 1965.